WRITING ARTICLES THAT SEL

G.J.MATSON

WRITING ARTICLES THAT SELL

I proudly dedicate this book to the
rabbit (name long since forgotten)
whose hutch inspired my first saleable
Manuscript

ISBN 0 906486 01 7

Writing School Guides published by
Clarefen Limited, 18–20 High Road, Wood Green,
London N22 6BX

Printed in Great Britain by
Billing and Sons Limited
Guildford, London and Worcester

Contents

Beginning at the Beginning

Funny how some incidents stick in the mind.

One I still remember, as if it were yesterday. I can see myself now — hurrying home from school, flinging my bicycle into the shed, racing into the house, and shouting "It's in! It's in!"

What the daily help thought of me I never stopped to consider. The way her eyes seemed to shoot from their sockets, however, clearly indicated that her feelings were far from normal.

The rest of the household, almost in unison, half rose from the tea-table and requested me to make less noise and to remember there was a distinguished visitor to tea.

Any anyhow, what was in? And in what?

With a flourish that would have done justice to a bogus company promoter spreading out the plans of a proposed new factory before the eyes of a gullible and monied audience, I opened out a copy of a two-penny gardening paper.

"There!" I exclaimed.

And the distinguished visitor, probably because he found the hospitality of my people so much to his liking, or, was anxious to show that he, at least, knew a genius when he met one, gave me a thump on the back and followed it up with a friendly, "Well done, lad".

1

What, you may ask, was the object which called forth such excitement, and the warm congratulations of a man of substance?

I will tell you.

In one corner of the paper was a short paragraph accompanied by an illustration in line, above which were the words "A Novel Rabbit Hutch"; and at the foot, "G.J. Matson".

A short time before, I had dared to send an unsolicited contribution to a London editor — and here it was in print.

My first submission, and my first acceptance!

In passing, let me mention that this first effort of mine, as I have since realised, found editorial favour because of two things: (a) it was practical, (b) it described something new. I have found since that articles of this kind are among some of the easiest to place, about which, more anon.

I happened to strike lucky with my first attempt. It may have been that I was born with the ability to write, and sell what I had written. I thought so myself — at that time. Spurred on by this initial success, I sat down and wrote a score or so other articles, all in a neat round schoolboy hand, and posted them off to editors whose addresses I found on the back pages of newspapers and magazines which reposed in the old-fashioned case by the side of the chiffonier (late nineteenth century for sideboard!).

In the meantime I received a small cheque for the rabbit hutch piece, and visions of easy money, and lots of it, began to float before my eyes. That, I am told, is the kind of experience which usually follows an early success!

But my hopes failed to materialise, and several years passed before I again saw my name in print. My second success, however, proved much more important than the first, and from that time, I began to make steady progress until finally

2

a wide free-lancing connection enabled me to throw up a safe job as an assistant master in a large boarding school, and rent an office within a few yards of the 'street of ink'. Or, as — in my opinion — Philip Gibbs more aptly described it, 'The Street of Adventure'.

But to revert to my second success. It happened in this way.

One day I confiscated a copy of a boys' magazine (which has now, unhappily, ceased publication) from one of the pupils in my class who seemed to find it far more entertaining than the French irregular verbs I had set him to learn. At the time, I was just getting interested in photography and, glancing through the magazine which had fallen into my hands — strange how these confiscated papers often prove as irresistible to the master as to the pupil — the thought struck me that the magazine's readers might possibly be interested in a series of short, simple, articles dealing with the use of a camera.

Accordingly, I drafted a suitable letter, outlining my idea in full, and sent a typed copy to the editor without delay. It must have been just the feature for which he was looking. Within a few days a reply came back asking me to prepare eight articles as soon as possible. This I did, and the series began to appear in print. Before it was half way through, the editor wrote to me again. It was, he said, so popular that he would like to continue it. Could I prepare a further nine articles? Could I! Before the week was out they were in the post, and every Saturday morning for seventeen weeks I received a useful cheque.

That success brought in its train the genuine writing bug, and I was bitten badly. I got down to business in real earnest. I read every book and article on the subject I could lay my hands on. I studied carefully every newspaper and magazine that came within my reach. And I analysed my failures in an effort to find out why they had failed.

Do not imagine, gentle reader, that the road to full-time free-lancing was easy after that second success. It was nothing of the kind. It meant six years of plodding, working up reliable connections, before I could hang my gown on the door for the last time and say good-bye to school and to the boys who preferred penny dreadfuls to French and Latin verbs.

It may be the ambition of many who read this book to make writing their sole means of livelihood.

A word to the wise.

Charles Lamb has said that 'literature is a bad crutch but a very good walking stick'. There is a good deal of truth in that, and I would strongly advise anyone not to give up safe employment until he has evidence that he can write well enough to sell articles regularly.

It is not enough to have the urge to write. You cannot live on enthusiasm. What you think and feel you could do if you had more time matters little. It is success in cash terms that must be the only deciding factor.

If, in your spare time, you are able to knock up saleable articles with pleasing regularity, and can number among your friends a score or so of editors who take nearly everything you send them, then you can start to think about devoting the whole of your time to writing.

Let me say that once you reach that happy stage, there is no life more attractive or more exciting. You are free to go your own way. Every experience is an adventure — and one which can probably be turned into hard cash.

I number among my friends a few free-lance journalists whose yearly average income from full-time writing is very attractive. They would not swop places with the man in

4

industry who probably earns more. On the other hand, I know many writers who earn a couple of hundred pounds a year from writing in their spare time. They would not throw up a safe job for any sum they might earn from their pens. And I do not blame them!

Some of us, you see, are born gamblers; others prefer a bird in the hand to a dozen in the bush.

DOES INFLUENCE COUNT?

No!

Despite what ninety-nine out of a hundred beginners think, and say, the answer is still — No!

Consider, for a minute, the business of publishing. Why do men and women put their money into a publishing business? To lose it? "Absurd" you say. Yet that is precisely what you imply if you are one of those who assert that the way to success in authorship is to be found through the channel of influence.

Publishers, like other sensible business men, sink their capital in publishing with the sole idea of making it pay dividends. And they know that the only way in which this result can be achieved is by 'delivering the goods'.

Why do you purchase a newspaper or a magazine? Only because the items in it are likely to entertain, amuse, or educate you. You do not buy a paper because its publisher has purchased a manuscript from one of his friends, or from a friend's friend. You buy a paper or a magazine on its 'track record'. Because you believe it likely to fulfil your expectations.

It is true that editors often go out for big names. But why?

Influence? Nothing of the kind. Editors know that big names have a large following of readers, and that circulations — the average editor's nightmare — are often affected appreciably by the habit readers have of following their favourite writers. But how did these names become so famous? It needs but a small intellect to grasp the truth. Which is, that they owe their following entirely to the fact that they have the ability to write matter which a large section of the public is anxious to read, and to deliver it on time.

So you see, this influence bogey is all eyewash!

Have you read the life story of the late Lord Northcliffe? If not, do so: it will encourage you. He started work when most boys are still at school; he had no money, and there were no kind friends to give him introductions to benevolent editors. Yet, by sheer hard work and an indomitable courage, he quickly rose to the proprietorship of *The Times*, *Daily Mail*, *Evening News* and other national papers.

You may not be a Northcliffe, but at the commencement of your career it is as well to foster two, at least, of the qualities which characterized this great journalist. Namely, a desire to work hard, and the ability to smile at disappointments.

The latter is important. In no profession does fate hand out so many hard knocks as in that of writing. It is only fair to add, however, that, conversely there are many surprises. But without the ability to withstand the former, you are not likely to meet with many of the latter.

At the beginning of this section, I stated emphatically that influence does not count. Let me now qualify this statement just a little. It can count — but not until you have proved you can 'deliver the goods'.

When you have made friends with a number of editors, and

have shown that you can be relied upon to write good articles in an entertaining way, you will find that one may mention your name to another.

Or, if you meet one of your editor friends, personally, and he is in the company of another editor, he may introduce you and tell his friend what 'a good chap you are'.

Or, when you go to interview an editor, you may be able to say that such and such an editor has known you for a number of months and that you have had the pleasure of writing a good many articles for his paper. That fact may make a good impression on the editor you are interviewing, and he will most likely think that if your work is good enough for such and such a paper, it will, without a doubt, be suitable for his.

Since I started writing this book a friend has mentioned my name to an editor who works in the same office. On this recommendation alone, the editor has written and asked me to prepare two illustrated articles. In his letter the editor says: "I was thinking of getting the photographs taken myself, but Mr. - - - tells me you can handle this part of the work as well. I will, therefore, leave them to you and should like four or five for each article".

This last paragraph will show you how important it is to get on friendly terms with editors — and as quickly as you can. Do not, however, make the fatal mistake of pushing yourself on them.

By all means call on an editor if you get half a chance, but when you go, make sure you have one or two sound ideas to put before him. Talk to him in a business-like manner and let him see you are keen and anxious to make headway. But do not talk too much. Listen to what he has to say. I have never been to see an editor yet without coming away with ideas for at least one or two saleable articles.

7

I get a kick out of picking editors' brains! You can do the same.

CAN ANYONE LEARN HOW TO WRITE SALEABLE ARTICLES?

This is a natural question to ask. It is one I have been asked hundreds of times. And the answer is — No!

I know there are many people who genuinely think that anybody can be taught to produce saleable material, providing they follow certain definite rules of procedure. For myself, I think it is foolish to imagine that everyone can be made to write saleable articles. Many cannot even compose a decent letter; and many more cannot express a thought in simple language which is easy to understand.

Quite a number of people who have no real desire to write, look on writing as an easy way of getting a little extra pin-money. They imagine that they have only to write something, and there is an editor somewhere who will be willing to purchase what they have written. This type of person never gets far — if, in fact, he gets anywhere at all.

The great thing is to have the urge to write. This is the acid test. No one can be taught article writing who does not feel that he must write. If you feel this way, there is no reason why you should not quickly learn to arrange and relate facts in a saleable form. Read all you can about writing in books and suitable magazines, and by all means enrol for a course with a reputable correspondence school providing, of course, you are prepared to work hard and conscientiously.

The very fact that you are reading this book goes a long way to show that you have this necessary urge within you.

Follow carefully, then, the hints and suggestions in the pages that follow, and success may soon be yours.

WORK SYSTEMATICALLY

Before going more deeply into the subject of this book, I want to impress upon you the need for working systematically.

You will not get very far unless you do this. No matter whether you want to make free-lancing a whole-time job or only a profitable hobby — you must work to some sort of time table.

Try to write something every day. Even five minutes' work is better than none. If you can think of nothing else to write about, sit down and fill a page describing the antics of your dog or the habits of your wife.

If the urge to write is really in you, you will not mind writing every day, and as the habit grows, so will you come to derive more and more pleasure from it.

Take a piece of white card and print on it, in block letters: I MUST WRITE SOMETHING EVERY DAY. Pin the card over your desk and let it serve as a constant reminder that success depends very largely upon your putting this suggestion into practice.

Take no notice of those who tell you that it is impossible to write unless you feel like it. If your own mind suggests the thought, ignore that too. It is nonsense. Many writers have found they produce their best work when they drive themselves to it. After all, it is only a matter of concentration. When you have taught yourself to concentrate you will find it possible to work at any time and in any place.

How, do you think, would newspaper reporters fare if they

had to wait for inspiration before writing and sending in their copy? Or if they had to seek the comfort of an easy chair or the seclusion of a study before they could put their thoughts on paper? We should soon be reading news a week old.

At first a reporter does not find it easy to write at any time and in any place, but by forcing himself to it he soon acquires the art, and his writing suffers little in consequence.

Train yourself to work in the same way and not only will your output be increased, but your income will go up as well.

You will find that you will write and sell more if you are tidy. Too many freelances have untidy desks, littered with papers of all kinds; and too many waste hours having to look for odd pieces of information they require from stacks of papers stored haphazardly in a drawer or a cupboard.

Let me explain, briefly, how I work myself. This may help you. I have separate classified files for press-cuttings, negatives and photographs, and market information. I shall be referring to each of these later in the book.

I also have another file close beside me whenever I am working, and this gives me easy access to matters relating to all the work I have on hand at the moment. For this file I use sheets of cardboard (which can always be purchased from any printer), measuring 16 ins. wide by 10 ins. deep. These sheets are then folded down the middle to make useful containers, and a note of the matter to which the folder refers is made at the top. A number of these folders are permanent but others change from time to time.

If I give rough details of the file at present in use, it will help you to understand better how I work.

"Awaiting Attention" contains details (letters, and so on) which need seeing to in the near future; "Addresses" contains addresses which I am constantly using; "Awaiting Reply" is obvious; "Halloween" contains material for an article I am now writing; "Ideas" contains rough notes on ideas which have come to me but which I am not ready to use; "Inn Signatures" contains matter relating to an article I am now preparing on Inn Signs; "Juvenile Puzzle Book" deals with a children's book which is now being considered by Warne & Co; "Letters of Acceptance" is obvious; "Preliminary Letters" contains carbons of all the preliminary letters I send to editors; "Pub Stories" contains material I am collecting for a small book; "Sheer Guts Got Women into Medicine" refers to an article I am preparing giving the story of the first woman who became a doctor; "Stories for Speakers" contains material for a book I am now writing; "Writing Articles That Sell" covers matter relating to this present book; and so on.

Usually I have three covers for each book on which I am working — one for general matter, one for the typed original, and the other for the carbon copy.

I have two other covers in my current file of a rather special nature. They are concerned with markets for each of which I write a monthly article but, since neither has openings for general material, there would be no purpose in mentioning them by name. In connection with one of them, however, this little experience may prove interesting.

I was staying with a business friend some time ago when I was shown a long duplicated list of prices and special offers which were sent out every week by a London firm of wholesale grocers, to all its customers. I thought that a short article of general interest might help to make this list more attractive and I accordingly sent my suggestion to the Company.

The directors liked the idea but did not feel they could include an article in each list. They did ask me, however, to supply one for use once a month, and for some years now I

11

have been sending them about a page and a half of single spaced typing for which they have been paying me regularly.

My contribution deals with current affairs, gardening hints, topical notes, a humorous story or two, and so on. Years ago I supplied short items of general interest to a large firm in Cambridge for inclusion in a printed monthly price list which they sent to all their customers. It is well worth keeping an eye open for small outlets of this kind and I pass the idea on as a suggestion.

So much for systematic working. I want to add a final word urging you also to be tidy in your work.

You will know that articles should always be typed, in double spacing, on large post 4to or A4 paper. It is advisable to keep your manuscripts tidy, and as free from alterations as possible. Do not make a lot of pen alterations, as some writers do. I have seen some manuscripts where it is evident that the writer has just typed out a first draft of what he wanted to say and has then revised it with a pen and sent the untidy result off to an editor.

Editors are only human, and they will look more kindly at a neat manuscript than at one which is difficult to read because of many alterations.

FINDING MARKETS

You may wonder why I am dealing with this subject now, before dealing with the one in the next section. It may seem odd that we should deal with markets before having anything to sell. It seems contrary to all the accepted practices of everyday business. The average business man designs and produces a product before he goes out to find customers to buy it.

I am of the opinion that assembling an extensive and reliable file of market information, is the most important thing in the freelance armoury. Build up a file of this kind in a small filing cabinet, with an alphabetical index, using small filing cards. You can then paste short cuttings on the cards as you find them and add other relevent facts in ink as you come across them, or whenever a letter from an editor contains some useful information.

Try to get to know as much about every publication as you possibly can. I do not mean by this, of course, that you should try to get a close knowledge of every newspaper and magazine that is published. Rather keep to those which deal with subjects in which you are interested, and which publish articles of a kind which you think you might be able to write.

For myself, I have no interest in mechanics, and am not in the least mechanically minded. All publications of this kind, therefore, are out as far as I am concerned. I could mention many similar subjects which do not appeal to me, and which I therefore do not trouble to explore.

Let us see, then, how you can amass the necessary information. First of all there are the Reference Books and of these Writers and Artists Year Book, published by Adam and Charles Black, 4, 5 and 6, Soho Square, London, W.1. should always be by your side. It contains the requirements of scores of newspapers, magazines, book publishers, and so on.

The Newspaper Press Directory, published by Benn Brothers Ltd., Sovereign Way, Tonbridge, Kent, is a far more ambitious production, and although it costs considerably more, it is well worth having at hand. I have found it extremely useful in my own work. Although it lists a very large number of publications, no indication of their requirements is given, but if one looks as though it might be a

13

possible market, it is easy to send for a specimen copy and study it. I have found many new markets by doing just this.

Next I would mention *Writers' Monthly* a periodic professional Magazine published from P.O. Box 34, St. Andrews, Fife, KY16 9AF. This is a must for all who are interested in writing. It is a mine of up to the minute market information. In between issues of Writers and Artists Year Book so many requirements change. A subscription to Writers' Monthly is the sure way to keep bang up to date.

A good way to get advance news of all new books is to subscribe to *The Bookseller,* which you can order through your newsagent or obtain direct by post from 12 Dyott Street, London WC1A 1DF. For periodicals and an up-to-the-minute glimpse of the fast-changing paperback scene one should regularly read *Newsagent and Bookshop,* again available locally or direct from Haymarket Publishing Limited, Regent House, 54-62 Regent Street, London W1A 2YJ.

Your local Public Library is a good place for studying a number of different magazines, and when you are in a strange town, and have a few minutes to spare, it is a good plan, too, to visit the Public Library there. If you are on holiday and it is wet, you may easily spend a profitable hour or two browsing in the magazines in the Library of the town in which you are staying. Different libraries often display different sets of publications.

Another good idea is to make friends with your local newsagent, so that he will let you glance through the magazines in his shop from time to time. You can always purchase any that have a particular appeal to you and take them away for a more leisurely study at home.

When visiting the houses of friends, always keep an eye open for any magazines they may have which are not particularly known to you. I have often found a publication of this kind which has led to an acceptance later.

These are just a few ways of getting hold of market information. File it away as I have suggested and try to keep as much of it in mind as possible. Then, when you get an idea, you will immediately think, "that should suit so-and-so", and you can start working on it accordingly.

FINDING IDEAS

We are now ready to be thinking of suitable ideas and, having found them, we can go on to consider how best to prepare them and present them to a likely editor for publication.

Before you begin to write an article you must have an idea. An idea is the first requisite to successful writing. You haven't any? Well, get one! How? I will try and show you.

In the first place, think of yourself. Interview yourself. What are your interests? What people have you known? What trips have you taken? What exciting things have happened to you? What are your Hobbies? Dozens of ideas will spring from your answers to these questions, and the more you think about them, the more you will discover in the way of ideas.

Hobbies are a great source of inspiration, and since most are catered for by magazines confined exclusively to matter relating to them, the possible field for articles is a wide one. Examples of magazines which fall into this class are:- Aero-modeller, Amateur Gardener, Amateur Photographer, Amateur Winemaker, British Chess Magazine, Caravan, Chess, Dog News, Golf World, Model Aircraft, Our Dogs, Philatelic Magazine, Popular Gardening, Stamp Magazine, Yachting World, and so on. If you have taken a genuine interest in any of the

15

hobbies covered by these papers, you should be able to write at least a few short articles around experiences connected with them.

Articles on hobbies need not be confined, however, to the hobby press. Openings exist in all the national leading provincial newspapers, as well as in juvenile magazines and annuals, and many of the domestic weeklies. It is possible, for instance, to sell articles on photography to many different newspapers and magazines; and stamp articles sometimes crop up in the most unlikely places.

Some hobbies have not a wide enough interest, or do not carry sufficient advertising possibilities, to make the publication of a magazine of their own a commercial proposition. Articles dealing with such hobbies, however, frequently find their way into the pages of suitable magazines.

Examine your hobbies from all possible angles. If you collect coins, for instance, you need not confine your writing to articles about the actual collection of them, the groups into which they fall, and so on. Quite an interesting article could be written about the different metals they contain, another about their shapes, and a third about the inscriptions on them.

One of my own hobbies for several years, has been stamp collecting, and I have been able to place a number of articles on this subject in many different markets. At one time, the thought struck me that an article, or perhaps even a series of articles, could be written on the subject which forms the major part of the design of some of the world's best known stamps. There is the Kookaburra bird common on Australian stamps, for example; the air adventures of Santos Dumont which are featured on Brazilian stamps; the United Empire Loyalists to be found on Canadian Stamps, and so on.

I could soon see that it would be a fairly easy matter to get

16

a mass of material along these lines, and I thought it would be a pity to packet it up into a number of short articles. Why not put the lot together and make a book? This I did. I sent my manuscript, entitled *Stamps With a Story*, to Blackie & Son, and it was accepted and published straight away. In passing, I might mention that whenever you have accumulated a lot of material on one particular subject, it is always worth considering if it could be made up into a book.

It is easy to turn from hobbies to games. Here again, endless opportunities exist and there are scores of papers which cater for national sports. As with hobbies however, the writer need not confine his articles on sports to these magazines. He may tackle the London and provincial newspapers, as well as many weekly and monthly magazines of a general nature.

Unless you are a first-class player, or well known in connection with any particular game, do not write articles on how to play. Editors will not be a bit interested in them if you do. The only exception is when writing for juvenile markets, then you may try your hand at instructional articles.

Instead, approach the game from a new angle. As an example, let us consider tennis for a moment and see how this game might be approached. What is tennis played with? A racket and ball. Very well, why not an article describing how tennis balls are made, and another how rackets are made? Well illustrated, both these articles should sell easily. And what about choosing a racket? There are surely several useful hints regarding this which could be passed on to beginners.

When was tennis first played? Have the rules changed much? Is it played differently in any countries abroad? How did the players of the last generation differ from the players of this? (A chat with your grandmother is indicated here!).

How does one set about forming a tennis club? What are

17

the officers of a tennis club expected to do? How are tournaments arranged? These are subjects worth writing up, and they do not by any means exhaust the possibilities.

Let us now turn from ourselves and our own interests to other people and their interests. It is said that every person can tell at least one good story. Endeavour, then, to get a story from every person you meet. This is not as difficult as it may seem if you bear in mind the fact that the story is likely to be connected with the person's chief interests.

Take, for example, the gamekeeper. Two or three chats with one of these worthies will provide material for a dozen articles. His work alone is interesting, but is seldom written about. Apart from his actual work, however, consider his knowledge of wild animal life. Hundreds of newspapers and magazines are interested in articles on this subject. He will probably never write a single article himself, but, if approached in a courteous manner, he will be glad to relate the more interesting of his experiences to an open-eared freelance. He may also be able to suggest numerous photographic studies, few of which the freelance would stumble across in the ordinary way.

You may think I have mentioned a gamekeeper because he provides a particularly good example. Not a bit of it. The postman who drops your letters through the door, or the dustman who collects your refuse, are just as suitable. The great thing is to get them talking about something which interests them — and then leave them to ramble on.

I can give you a very good personal example of the sort of thing I mean. I have never been to the Antarctic, and I know I shall never go. Nevertheless, I am at the present time able to write a number of authentic articles about the subject. I have a young nephew who has been on three expeditions to the

Antarctic. When he was home after his second expedition, he called to see me for a few hours, told me of some of his experiences, and showed me many of the photographs he had taken.

I saw at once that here was the chance of selling several well-illustrated features, and we agreed at once that if he supplied the material and photographs, I would write up the articles and place them. A split of 50/50 in respect of the proceeds received seemed fair to both of us.

It was not long after this that I had sold articles to *Ashore and Afloat, Nautical Magazine* and *Dog's Bulletin* to mention but a few. When he went back on his third expedition, I gave him precise details of the sort of material which would be saleable, and also made suggestions for photographs which would be worth taking. When he gets back I have no doubt we shall be successful in selling more features, and we are also considering the possibility of preparing a well-illustrated book based on his experiences.

Another source of ideas is the newspaper. Many writers find that this source alone is sufficient to keep them working at full pressure, without searching for ideas in any other direction.

When I have finished reading my morning newspaper in the ordinary way, I go through it again looking for ideas. I do the same with nearly every magazine I read. I make a note of every paragraph which suggests an idea and commence to follow up any which seem to offer immediate possibilities.

Here are just two examples of what can happen. Some years ago, when new five pound notes were issued, the newspapers gave a report of the girl who was chosen to be the model for the picture of Britannia featured on them. Using this news in a topical opening paragraph, I then followed on with the story of the woman who is seen as Britannia on some of our coinage.

The result was an article of some 500 words which was accepted by *Reveille*. Again, later, a newspaper item told me that the Bath Festival was featuring a special exhibition of baths going back thousands of years. Using this information as a topical opening, I wrote a long article on bathing through the ages in general, and of the bathing habits of women in particular. This went off to a leading London Syndicate.

It would be possible for me to give scores of examples like these, but these are sufficient to show how a newspaper can suggest an idea, and how the idea can be written up and turned into cash (which, I presume, is what every reader of this book is after!)

The correspondence columns of newspapers are always worth a careful study. Many of the letters published contain ideas for articles and additional facts can often be obtained by writing direct to addresses given at the foot of them. I would also mention, in passing, that correspondence columns sometimes afford a handy means of obtaining information. More than once, when I have wanted certain facts to complete an article, I have written to one of the national newspapers and within an issue or two some reader has satisfied my needs.

Some time ago I read an article which dealt with methods of creating ideas. I have never found it necessary to experiment with any of these methods myself, but they struck me at the time, as being promising ones.

One of these, I remember, was to write down a number of stock 'forms' of titles and to juggle with them until a suitable subject suggested itself. Here are some suggested forms: "How to —"; "— something to"; "Too many —"; "Choosing a —". Having made a list, the method consists of replacing the blanks by suitable verbs or nouns. Thus we might get: "How to reseat a chair"; "Teaching a puppy to eat"; "Too many holidays";

and "Choosing a hobby". Any of these subjects might make a saleable article.

Ideas can sometimes be found when you are listening to the radio or watching a television programme. Here is an example. A short time ago I was watching "Zoo Time" on the television when Dr. Desmond Morris introduced the Caracal Lynx 'Gigi'. In the course of conversation, he mentioned that this particular animal had been presented to the Society by H.R.H. King Hussein of Jordan.

I immediately thought that a good article could be written about the various animals which have been presented to the Zoo by members of our own Royal Family, as well as by members of Royal Families abroad. I wrote to the Press Department of the Zoological Society at Regents Park and asked if they could give me any details along these lines. In reply, they sent me a mass of interesting material, concerning various animals, and I was able to write up an article and sell it to *The Guide,* the official organ of the Girl Guides Association.

Ideas beget ideas. Let me show you what I mean. A short time ago I had a cold. (Nothing original about that). My throat was sore and I was given certain home-made drinks to relieve the irritation. Splendid! They worked! So I thought, "What is good for me may be good for others. Why not an article on Drinks that Comfort Colds?" I set to work on the idea and within a few days had sold the article to the Home Page editor of a Provincial Newspaper.

I did not finish there, however. Toying further with the idea, I thought, "Why not an article on home-made drinks? Or, better still, home-made wines?" Properly written, and submitted at the right time, this will certainly sell to the editor of a home page.

Wines led me to think of grapes. There must be an

21

interesting story connected with the harvesting of grapes. I have never seen an article on it and I have made up my mind to find out where, and when, this takes place on a large scale. If I am able to get hold of some suitable illustrations, I may quite easily be able to prepare and sell two or three different articles on this subject.

And what of grapes? "Can they" I thought, "be used for any other purpose than for dessert and the making of wine? Can they be used in connection with cooking for instance?" I must jot this idea on my list and endeavour to find out.

Do you see now how easy it is to find subjects, once you let your mind run in the right channels? I think you do.

PRELIMINARY LETTERS

We have now seen how we can find ideas, and we must go on to concern ourselves with turning these ideas into manuscripts and selling them. Let me emphasize here, however, that the idea itself is all important. At this stage it does not matter at all if you do not have sufficient material from which to write up an article of a suitable length. In a later section I shall explain how you can quite easily obtain material, and also photographs, for almost any idea you may have.

It may seem a bit like putting the cart before the horse when I say that you should now try to get an editor interested in your idea before you have actually written the manuscript. This, however, is a good idea as I am sure you will find when you start to gain a little experience.

How can you get editors interested in ideas? By sending out what are known as 'preliminary letters'. During practically the whole of my free-lancing career, I have made a practice of not submitting an article to an editor, who has not already accepted some of my work, and with whose general editorial policy I am not familiar, until I have first paved the way for it by sending a preliminary letter. I am convinced it is chiefly due to this that I have been able to work up a connection with such a large number of newspapers and magazines.

Perhaps you are wondering just what a preliminary letter is. Let me give you an example.

Supposing you have in mind an article of about 1000 words, illustrated by two or three photographs, on the subject: "Deserted and Forgotten Churches". It is the type of article, you think, which would appeal to the Editor of a Church Magazine. Very well, do not submit the article straight away but, in the first place, send a preliminary letter worded somewhat as follows:

Dear Sir,

I am wondering if you could care to consider an article of about 1000 words in length, on the subject of "Deserted and Forgotten Churches". I have got together a good deal of interesting matter on this subject, which I feel would prove entertaining to your readers.

Suitable illustrations would accompany the article.

Thanking you for your kind consideration, and awaiting your reply with interest.

I remain,

Yours truly,

Enclose a stamped addressed envelope with your letter, and in due course you will receive a reply. If this is favourable, you can prepare and submit your manuscript. If an editor does express a willingness to see your article, you are more than half way to success, and if it should eventually come back, you will know that the fault is yours in the presentation of it.

Perhaps your actual writing is not good enough or you have not been able to get together material which is strong enough.

Many beginners have an idea that editors do not welcome preliminary letters. Let me dispel this notion. In the whole of my experience I have found only two editors who have definitely discouraged the practice. One of these has since ceased to be an editor and the other wrote to the effect that he was "pleased to see any articles submitted to him". (Which might, of course, have been a gentle hint that he was not very interested in anything I was able to submit!)

Perhaps I have been more fortunate than other free-lances who have resorted to this practice. If so, it is, I think, because I have been careful of two things: (1) not to submit hackneyed ideas: and (2) to make certain an idea is suitable for the paper to which it is sent.

I once had an article on the subject of preliminary letters published in a magazine, widely read by writers. After it had appeared, a reader wrote to the editor as follows:

"This may be your contributor's experience in the later stages of his career. It is doubtful if a free-lance feeling his way would discover a preliminary letter to be helpful.

"If he writes to ascertain whether a particular article will be acceptable, the chances today are ten to one on his being told that the subject is already covered, that the topic is hackneyed, or that the contribution will be unacceptable for one of a dozen other reasons."

The same thought may suggest itself to some readers of this book. If it suggests itself to you — forget it! No editor — and note the emphasis on the 'no' — will turn down a good idea because he has never heard of the writer who suggests it. On the contrary, he will be more likely to encourage such a writer. Good ideas are too scarce to be treated lightly.

The advantages of sending preliminary letters are many.

In the first place, I have found that when an editor has to turn down an idea he may be kind enough to suggest another. A good example of this occurred to me only a few months before writing this book.

I approached the editor of a certain magazine with the idea for an article dealing with the training of guide dogs for the blind. He replied to the effect that he could not ask me to prepare an article on these lines, because the subject was already partly covered in a serial story he was running. Then he went on to ask: "Could you let me have an article on Cruft's Dog Show?" I got on to this article straight away, submitted it, and within a few days had a letter with an offer for it.

If I had submitted my article on guide dogs in the first place, the chances are that it would have been returned with an ordinary rejection slip, and the opportunity of preparing something on Cruft's Dog Show would not have presented itself.

It must not be overlooked that there are several reasons, other than unsuitability, which may cause a manuscript to be rejected. Seldom, however, will an editor give a reason on a rejection slip; but when replying to a preliminary letter, he is almost compelled to state one.

It sometimes happens that he has already used an article on similar lines, or has one ready for use. For instance, I once suggested to the editor of *Territorial Magazine* an illustrated article on troops used in the making of films.

The editor replied to the effect that he had published an article on the same subject in the current issue. I might have wasted much valuable time preparing this article, and the sole reason for its rejection would have been the fact that it clashed with one in print.

Sometimes I have found that when an editor has been compelled to turn down a suggestion because he has already used something on the same subject recently, he will suggest that I approach him again in, say, six months' time and then tackle the subject from a different angle. I have sold scores of articles in this way, and I cannot think that I should have sold any of them if I had relied on rejection slips.

Again, an editor may be full up with material for some months ahead. He is not likely, however, to give this information on all the rejection slips sent out, but he is certain to give it in reply to a preliminary letter.

Apart from very short articles, topical articles, and articles for markets I know very well, I never submit an article until an editor has expressed a willingness to consider it. If, after that, it comes back, I know that the reason for rejection is entirely with myself, and if the editor has not already done so for me, in a covering letter, I immediately post mortem my manuscript in an endeavour to find out exactly why it has failed.

COLLECTING MATERIAL

Once you have hit upon an idea for an article worth writing up, and have sent off a preliminary letter in connection with it, the next thing is to start looking around for suitable material with which to fill the article. Let us see how this is done.

In the first place there is your own personal experience. You may know a little bit about the subject and, if you do, you can jot it down on a piece of paper as a start.

Then you can refer to press cuttings on the subject and these will probably prove very useful. Later on I shall be explaining how to build up a press cutting file of your own and, as this grows, you will find more and more material always ready at hand.

In the meantime, there are countless organisations willing to help free-lance writers in the preparation of articles and news stories. At different times I have made use of several of these, and I recall numerous articles which would never have been written but for their kindly aid.

To give particulars of all these organisations would fill a small book. I have already mentioned the Zoological Society and the help which it gave me in the preparation of one particular article. This is a good example of what can be done.

Let me digress here a moment and say that it pays all free-lances to get a copy of the London Telephone Directory and also of the London Classified Telephone Directory. Wherever you live you can obtain copies of both of these by applying to your local Telephone Exchange and, if you are yourself a subscriber, the cost can be added to your account. Both can be obtained very cheaply, and they are well worth the expense.

In the former, of course, you can find the address of any Association, Club, or business concerns you are anxious to trace. The latter is rather different in that it contains all these addresses, and many others, in a classified alphabetical form. Thus, for example, there is a section devoted to Button Merchants, containing a score or two of firms which manufacture buttons; another entitled Clock Makers and Importers, containing another score or two of names; Furniture Manufacturers, containing rather a long list of names, Paper Makers; Protective Clothing, and so on.

Whatever kind of article you are writing, you are almost certain to find places in one or other of these directories to which you can write for information and photographs. The latter can be a veritable gold mine of ideas in itself, containing, as it does, such a wide range of varied subjects.

This Classified Directory has helped me on innumerable occasions and I should not like to be without it. Here are a few examples of how I have found it useful.

A few weeks ago I came across a market note concerning the requirements of the *Gliksten Journal*, published as a House Journal by a large firm of Timber Merchants. Although the Editor is, obviously, mainly concerned with articles about wood or timber products, he does also find openings for articles which have only a remote interest in wood.

Acting on this information, I wrote suggesting an article on match-making which I proposed calling "From Tree to Match". The Editor replied that he had published an article on this subject in a recent issue and he kindly sent me a copy of the issue containing the article. If I had anything different to offer, he said he might possibly use it in a later issue.

In the circumstances I thought it better to keep away from matches for the time being, and then I thought that the majority of inn signs are made of wood, and using this brief connection in an opening paragraph, I wrote an article on the history of inn signs in general. The Editor liked my article and asked for some suitable illustrations. I had none.

Turning to the Classified Directory I looked up the section devoted to Brewers and wrote off to three or four firms asking if they could supply me with suitable illustrations. I soon had twenty or so, and from these the Editor was able to select a number which interested him.

At this point I would say that when you send for photographs of this kind, you never quite know what you are going to get and, often, the photographs you receive suggest

28

ideas for other articles. In this case, for example, I received a very fine photograph of the "Five Alls" sign which is probably one of the rarest in the country. A short article about this sign, accompanied by the photograph, made another acceptable feature.

Again, amongst the photographs received from another firm was a very attractive one of "The Black Dog and Duck Inn" at Bury in Sussex, and this appears to be one of the few inns which does not carry a visible sign. It dates back to 1560, and is one of the very few remaining thatched inns in the country. This immediately gave me the idea for another saleable article.

When I was writing my last batch of Christmas articles I had one dealing with the story of the Christmas Card and another dealing with Christmas Crackers. From the directory I obtained lots of material and some useful sets of photographs from firms listed under the appropriate headings.

Recently I have sold an illustrated feature to *Home Owner* dealing with candlelight in the home, and for this I was able to obtain a good deal of information, and a fine set of photographs from Price & Co. I have enough photographs over to make an attractive Christmas article under the subject "Dining by Candlelight".

Another subject I have dealt with recently is Wildfowl Reserves, and by writing to the Nature Conservancy I was able to get a useful list of these reserves, from many of which I was able to obtain much useful information and I sold an article on the subject. Amongst the illustrations I supplied when selling the piece was one of a raft providing space for nesting birds on some flooded gravel pits in a privately owned reserve in Kent. The Owner asked for a fee for the photograph, the proceeds going towards the upkeep of the reserve. I gladly agreed.

A few months ago I sold quite a number of articles about

Stately Homes — Woburn Abbey, Braemore House, Beaulieu Palace House, Ragley Hall, Hatfield House, and so on — and from each of these places I was able to get a good deal of information and literature, as well as some fine sets of photographs. I sold articles on various aspects of these subjects to such magazines as *Ford Times, C.G.A. Magazine, 600 Magazine,* and *Essex Countryside,* to mention but a few.

In passing, it might be observed that most counties today have their own County Magazine a rare list of which is given in the second book in this series of invaluable Workshop Manuals — *1,333 MARKETS.* The editors of these periodicals are always interested in any articles which have a direct bearing on their county. They nearly always, however, require a good selection of photographs from which they can choose a number for illustration purposes.

Another way in which you can get material for most of the articles you are writing, is by visiting the Public Library. The local Library is almost certain to contain some books having references to the subject on hand. Librarians are invariably courteous and willing to give careful attention to any genuine enquiry. They will answer queries by telephone and also send information by post.

It is my belief that the average writer does not make half as much use of the public library as he might. Yet it's shelves are teeming with ideas and material for countless articles. If space permitted I could mention scores of examples in support of this. Here is just one.

A short time ago I came across a book on Deserted and Forsaken Churches. Since it was over thirty years old, I first verified the facts contained in it, and then set out to visit some of the places mentioned and get suitable photographs of them. As a result I have since written three articles on the subject and have sufficient facts for at least two more.

If you are wanting any information about places or peoples overseas, do not forget the Embassies and London offices of the High Commissioners. I have received very useful help from many of these on many varying occasions.

Do not be afraid to go to anyone whom you think may be able to supply you with the facts you need. If you are writing an article about the Post Office, knock up a conversation with the postman; if it concerns fish, make friends with an angler, and so on. By doing this you will probably find that you will get more than sufficient facts for the article you have in mind. You may even get enough for a second, or perhaps a third.

A writer should never forget the other fellow. Get into conversation with as many people as you can. Tap the other person's mind. Drag from him as many interesting facts as you can and you will never lack a subject, and the material from which to write it up.

COLLECTING PRESS CUTTINGS

Before we see how we are actually going to write the article, let us consider for a minute or two, the way of building up a personal Press Cutting file. You will remember I referred to this briefly in the last section. The practice of building up such a file is undoubtedly of great value to the free-lance. The ways in which these cuttings may be used are many and the average free-lance will find that, as his collection grows, so will his output.

In the first place, cuttings are invaluable when it comes to topical articles. As witness an example.

Some years ago the leading newspapers published stories to

the effect that the Koebenhaven (a lost Danish training ship) had been sighted off Tristan da Cunha, that her helm was unmanned, and that apparently there was not a soul on board. It was, in fact, a mystery ship, and it seemed that an article dealing with similar mystery ships would, on account of its topicality, prove welcome to a London editor. Accordingly, I hunted up a batch of cuttings on "Ocean Mysteries" and immediately prepared a short article entitled "Ghost Ships of Many Seas". Within two days it appeared in a London newspaper.

If the cuttings had not been to hand, it would have been impossible to have prepared and submitted this article while the subject was still topical.

Cuttings are useful also for supplying the necessary material for anniversary articles. I refer here, of course, to annual events like New Year, Shrove Tuesday, Grand National, Boat Race, Ascot, Budget, Easter, and so on. These are all subjects which can be written up year after year, and the cuttings are collected to give an almost limitless number of ideas. I know of more than one colleague who has found it possible to devote the whole of his time to the writing of articles on these annual events.

Cuttings are useful, too, for providing inspiration for articles when otherwise inspiration seems dead. Many a time, in my early days, I was lost for a subject. I had only to glance through a few batches of cuttings, however, and a dozen or more workable ideas presented themselves to me. It is not wise, of course, to re-use the principal idea which any one cutting contains, unless you approach it from an entirely different angle, for this, surely, is a form of plagiarism.

It is generally possible to pick out one or two interesting facts from each of a number of cuttings and to put these together in the form of an entirely original manuscript which has no resemblance at all to any of the original articles from which the facts have been taken. I have resorted to this practice myself on innumerable occasions and the results have been so successful that I do not hesitate to pass the idea on.

If you decide to make a speciality of one or two particular subjects, a good collection of cuttings is absolutely essential if you are to be really successful. It is surprising how quickly you can build up a strong selection, on one particular subject, when you set your mind to the task. And it need hardly be added that all the time you are building up your collection you are getting a more thorough grounding in your subject and are frequently discovering suitable ideas for articles.

Having discovered some of the uses to which cuttings may be put, it will be interesting now to consider how they are obtained and how they may best be classified.

First of all, then, where to obtain them.

I do not buy many magazines regularly for the sole purpose of cutting. I have found, however, that some of the more popular weeklies — such as *Tit-Bits*, for example — are usually rich in suitable cuttings, and hardly a week passes, therefore, without some of these publications coming to the notice of my scissors. My daily papers (I always take two), also provide me with regular clippings. So does *Country Life*.

Whenever opportunity presents itself I visit auction sales or second-hand bookshops and look for magazines suitable for cutting. A few weeks before writing this book I picked up twenty-eight volumes of the *Strand Magazine*, dated round about 1900, for a very modest sum. From these I got over 100 first-class cuttings, and within a week one of them alone helped me to earn a useful fee amounting to many times what I had paid for all the books.

I have found, too, that one can pick up many useful cuttings at the expense of one's friends. Get to know what newspapers and periodicals they take regularly. If any of them are different from those you take yourself ask if you may have copies when they have finished with them.

Then there is the local library to consider. On enquiry you will find that used newspapers and magazines can often be purchased cheaply.

And now a word about classifying cuttings.

When I first began to collect, I made a number of folders from ordinary brown paper — as strong as I could get — and as cuttings were obtained, they were placed in the folders which bore titles most applicable to their subject-matter. It will be understood that this classifying was quite a crude arrangement, but I felt that, until I had a fair collection, it was as good as any.

The titles of the various folders, as near as I can remember them now, were Anniversaries, Natural History, Stage and Cinema, Religion, Celebrities, Unusual Experiences, History, Geography, Science, Art, Literature, Domestic Law, Handicrafts, Customs, Political and Miscellaneous.

As soon as a folder became uncomfortably full, I divided the cuttings again, this time into foolscap envelopes. Thus, Natural History was divided into Ants, Dogs, Elephants, Grouse, Mice, Rabbits, and so on. As time went on, all the folders became full and I now have some thousands of foolscap envelopes containing cuttings on as many subjects. These envelopes are arranged in alphabetical order and I am able to find information on any subject within a minute or two.

A few of the subjects, selected from my collection at random, may be of interest: Air Mails, Antipathies, Basket Making, Bibles, Careers for Boys, Chiropody, Corks, Dew

Ponds, Duels, Entertaining with Table Napkins, Foolhardy Feats, Giants and Dwarfs, Handwriting, Horse Brasses, Icebergs, Jest-books, Keeping Cool, Lightning, London Oddities, Marbles, Miniatures, Newspapers, Noses, Olive Harvests, Pacifism, Peat, Queen Elizabeth I, Refrigerators, Rings, Safe Deposits, Seaweed, Teasels, Unclaimed Fortunes, Valentine Day, Wassailing, Yom Kippur, and Zebras.

It will be seen from these examples that the range of subjects covered is a very wide one. It is because I collect cuttings on every subject I possibly can. It pays me to do so — and it will pay you.

WRITING THE ARTICLE

We can now assume that you have received an encouraging reply from an editor in answer to a preliminary letter, that you have collected together all the material you require, and that you are ready to go ahead with the writing of the article. Let us now consider how this is best done.

It is not too much to say that many would-be writers fail to get into print because they do not present their facts in proper order.

The best way I know of overcoming this is to draw up a skeleton outline of each article before attempting to write it. You will find this a first-rate exercise, and after a few attempts you will probably discover — as I have done — that you can do away with your paper outline; your facts marshal themselves in their proper order in your sub-conscious mind. Until this happens, however, stick to the skeleton.

For all practical purposes an article may be said to have three parts — the OPENING, the main facts forming the

BODY, and the ENDING.

For the OPENING try to get something topical or arresting; for the BODY obtain a number of striking and little-known facts; and for the ENDING find a fact which, in some way, is a little more striking than the rest.

You cannot pay too much attention to the opening paragraphs of your articles; and you must never forget that it is the duty of the last paragraph to round an article off so that it ends naturally and smoothly.

Let me give you some examples of good openings. Here are five:

1. 'Although you cannot possibly control the amount of dust that comes into your house, you can control, to a certain extent, the place where it collects."

(Article entitled: Dust on the Walls)

2. "A building that, when completed, will be one of the wonders of the world is being erected on a mountain side in America."

(Article entitled: House that Cannot be Destroyed)

3. "Many an insect which has stayed out too late, has been waylaid, robbed and destroyed by bandits on the look-out for unwary travellers. Their methods are many and varied, and some of them forestalled man in the use of bombs, gas and shooting."

(Article entitled: The Beetle Bandits)

4. "It is often urged by childless people that children are sure to come between husband and wife and upset a happy and smoothly working household."

(Article entitled: Quarrels Over the Children)

5. "Many and varied are the stains and marks that find their way on to the goods and chattels of the average household. Fortunately, the majority of them can be removed or at least

36

rendered much less conspicuous, if treated in the right way. Here is a selection of the most common stains and a few methods of treating them."

(Article entitled: Treating Stains)

There are two important points to notice about each of these openings. They are these (1) Each is arresting; (2) each introduces the subject straight away. No opening is good unless it embraces both of these points.

An editor is often compelled to read an article because the first few lines arouse his curiosity. If he fails to find anything interesting in the first paragraph, he may be tempted not to read any further. This will mean rejection.

It is a common fault to leave the introduction of a subject until the second or third paragraph. Do not let this fault be yours. It is very desirable, when you have to cram your facts into a few hundred words, to get right into the subject as quickly as possible.

Try to get something topical for your opening paragraph as often as you can. All editors are keen on topicality. Earlier in the book, I gave an excellent example of this when describing how I sold a quite general article following merely on a topical reference to the Britannia on a new issue of five pound notes.

So much for the opening.

The ending, I have said, must be natural and smooth. The aim should be to give the impression that you have said all there is to say about your subject and that, really, there is nothing more that can be said. Many of the manuscripts I have been asked to criticize have ended just where they were beginning to get interesting. This is a bad fault — but a very common one.

Pay special attention to the style of your ending. Coax it

to leave an impression on the mind like that left by a favourite sweetmeat on the tongue.

Now that your skeleton outline is worked out, you are ready to start writing. I expect many readers to register surprise when I say that the style of an article is by no means the most important thing about it.

Do not misunderstand me.

I do not mean by this that an editor ignores a writer's style. It is a fact, however, that those who are responsible for filling the magazine pages of newspapers, and those who edit the popular weeklies and monthlies, pay more attention to the actual subject-matter than to anything else. Make a note of this here and now. It does not matter how well you write — if you have nothing new or original to say you are wasting time by worrying an editor with your manuscript.

Do not force your style. Write naturally. In my early days the editor of a popular monthly gave me a piece of valuable advice which I have never forgotten. "To write a successful manuscript for an average publication," he said, "all you have to do is to write an ordinary letter on an interesting subject, and after writing it to cross out the 'Dear Sir' and 'Yours truly'."

Do not try to imitate the style of another writer, however successful he may be. If you write naturally, you will probably cultivate a style of your own, which will be just as pleasing.

Avoid overworked and misused words. The words definite and definitely, for instance, are often used unnecessarily. To write of 'a definite decision' is wrong, all decisions being definite. 'In few instances' is better replaced by 'seldom'; 'a degree of' means no more than 'some'; and 'largely' conveys the same meaning as 'in large measure'.

Say 'half' instead of 'fifty per cent'; 'man' or 'woman'

instead of 'person' or 'individual'; 'many' instead of 'numerous'; 'after' instead of 'subsequently to'; 'often' instead of 'frequently'.

It would be possible to fill several pages with similar examples, but those given are sufficient to show you what to guard against.

Most newspaper offices have a list of "Do's and Dont's" for use by regular correspondents and sub-editors. Here are a few extracts from such a book:

Avoid ending a sentence with etc. and however.

Don't use involved or inverted sentences. Aim at crispness and brevity.

Even the youngest babies have sex; don't annoy the mother by referring to her baby as 'it'.

Self-made men do not really 'begin life' as boot-blacks or pit-boys; say 'began to work as a boot-black'.

Avoid redundancies as in the following examples: Dead body, drowning fatality, surrounding circumstances, knots per hour (knots implies the time as well as the distance).

Never use a long word when a shorter one will do.

It is nice to have command over a large vocabulary and to be able to use more uncommon words than most of your fellows. The temptation to air them is great, but you must learn to withstand it. Many editors have assured me that the more simple the language, the better they like it.

Write so that anyone can understand what you have written. Be lucid. Study the works of Thomas Hardy and you will quickly see how attractive a simple style can be. The average reader gets no pleasure from an article if he is obliged to read it with a dictionary by his side.

Do not let these remarks, however, lead you to write articles which are made up of words of one or two syllables

39

only. If you do this your style will become flat and uninteresting. Vary the length of your words a good deal — but stick to words that are simple.

During my time I have criticized hundreds of articles, and I do not think I exaggerate when I say that more than half of them have contained sentences and paragraphs which were far too long. I have even read articles of 500 words in which there were no paragraphs at all! And it is quite common to find paragraphs, a page of typescript in length, which consist of one sentence only!

Perhaps this is a fault of which you have been guilty yourself. Take two or three of your rejected manuscripts and see how many sentences and paragraphs they contain. The examination will probably surprise you.

Generally speaking an article of 400 words should contain six or seven paragraphs and at least twice that number of sentences. This used not to be the rule a few decades ago. In the early part of the century, editors favoured long, drawn-out sentences and paragraphs. Now they are all in favour of the short sentence and paragraph.

If your sentences are short, your style becomes crisp. It is desirable that your style should be like this. Long sentences make for clumsiness. It must never be necessary for an editor to read a sentence twice before grasping its meaning. If he is a busy editor, he will not do it; he will probably send your manuscript back by the next post.

Never commence an article with a long sentence. Use a short sentence with plenty of punch. Follow it up with another short sentence and then if you like, introduce a longer one. Two short sentences to one long one is a good proportion and helps to balance an article. You must, however, vary the order. Otherwise your writing will become monotonous.

The same thing applies to paragraphs. If you vary the lengths of these, and do not make any unduly long, your article will have a more attractive appearance when in print.

The two most important parts of speech, where the writing of articles is concerned, are Verbs and Adjectives.

Let us deal with verbs first.

If you cast your mind back to your schooldays, and to the lessons in English Grammar, you will doubtless recall that verbs have VOICES. Of these there are two — Active and Passive.

What is the difference? Put into very simple language it is just this:

When <u>something is made to do something</u> the verb is said to be in the ACTIVE voice.

When <u>something has something done to it</u> the verb is said to be in the PASSIVE voice.

Notice particularly the words underlined and then consider these examples:

The dog chases the cat. What is happening here? The dog is doing something. It is chasing the cat. Therefore, it is the ACTIVE voice which is being used.

The cat is being chased by the dog. Here we have something different. This sentence does not tell us, in a direct manner, what something is doing (although, of course, we know by the sense of it) but, rather, what something is having done to it. The cat is being chased. The verb, therefore, is the PASSIVE voice.

Is this quite clear to you? If not, go over the above again, sentence by sentence, until you understand it thoroughly. It is important that you should do this. Why? Simply because editors always favour the Active Voice. If you would test the truth of this you have only to take up a few of the leading newspapers and magazines and read some of the articles printed in them.

It is easy to see why the Active Voice is favoured. It is more direct. It needs fewer words to describe the same fact. Both sentences given above as examples mean exactly the same, but while five words only are used in the first, eight are necessary in the second.

Use of the Passive Voice may help to spoil the chances of your manuscripts. If you make constant use of it editors will suspect you are still an amateur! And that they must never do.

Regarding adjectives, I would say just this: never use more than are necessary. One of the commonest faults beginners make, is to fill an article with unnecessary adjectives. It is a good plan to go through every finished article you write and strike out every adjective you possibly can. You will be surprised how this practice will improve your style.

Have you ever noticed how fresh a flower bed looks when you have weeded it? Your article may take on a similar freshness if you weed out the needless adjectives.

Select the adjectives you do use with care. Do not, for instance, write of a sudden arrival when what you really mean is an unexpected arrival. Remember that each adjective you use is directly connected with one particular noun. Consider, carefully, its connection with that noun before you allow it to stand.

There will always be a few writers who do not have to pay too much attention to punctuation. Their work being in such demand, editors will not mind punctuating it for them. Unfortunately many beginners imagine that they belong to this privileged class. Accordingly, they submit articles which are either abominably punctuated, or not even punctuated at all!

It will pay us to stop here for a minute, and consider the main rules which govern punctuation.

The full stop, colon and semi-colon, are used for the same purpose; namely, to separate portions of connected writing. Consider, for example, the following: "The clock struck twelve as he reached for the handle a shot rang out." Obviously, something is wrong here. The meaning is not clear. Introduce a full stop after twelve, however, and we understand exactly what the writer is trying to tell us.

The full stop and semi-colon are closely related. In all cases where a semi-colon is used a full stop could have been used if preferred. It should be remembered, however, that a full stop makes two separate statements stand out distinctly; whereas a semi-colon has the effect of linking them closely together. Thus the choice between the two often depends upon the shade of meaning desired.

The colon is always used when one statement formally introduces a second statement. Example: There is only one thing left to do: I must return.

A comma is used to separate parts of a sentence which, if no point were used, would be liable to misunderstanding. Consider, for instance, the following: "Seeing the men eating a woman the daughter of one of them went for some wine." Commas are evidently needed somewhere. Introduce them as follows, and the sentence is readily understood. "Seeing the men eating, a woman, the daughter of one of them, went for some wine."

When two or more adjectives are used to precede a noun, and are not joined by conjunctions, they should be separated by commas; but only if they are closely connected in meaning. If they are closely connected, no commas are necessary. The following are closely connected, and therefore, require commas: A strong, healthy girl. A round, smooth surface. These are not closely connected and, therefore, do not require commas: A rich young nephew. A large grey mare.

Two parts of a sentence, if joined by one of the common conjunctions — but, and, or, for, nor, or neither — should be separated by a comma. Example: The train moved slowly from the station, and the passengers took their seats.

Introductory phrases, used at the beginning of sentences, should be followed by a comma. Example: Although he was wet to the skin, he decided to go on.

Words like however, besides, therefore, etc. when coming at the beginning of sentences, should be followed by a comma. Example: However, you do as you please.

A short phrase of thinking, saying, and so on, coming at the end of a sentence, should be preceded by a comma. Example: You are right, I think.

A phrase of interrogation, coming at the end of a sentence is always preceded by a·comma. Example: That is correct, isn't it?

A quotation which is introduced by a verb of saying or thinking should be preceded by a comma. Example: He said, "I will."

Be careful not to use a comma when a full stop is obviously the only point which should be used. It is not correct, for instance, to write: "I ran to the station, it was too late to catch the train, but I knew the exercise would do me good." The part preceding the first comma is one distinct sentence; that following it is another. To be correct, therefore, we must write: "I ran to the station. It was too late to catch the train, but I knew the exercise would do me good."

Dashes and brackets are used to mark off phrases which, although forming part of a sentence, are not an essential part.

For example: He attempted to start the car for the purpose —
as he afterwards confided to me — of seeing if the self-starter
worked. If preferred, brackets could be used instead of the
dashes. Thus: He attempted to start the car for the purpose (as
he afterwards confided to me) of seeing if the self-starter
worked.

Expressions introduced by 'especially' and not preceded by
a conjunction are generally preceded by a dash. Example: He
likes fruit — especially apples.

A part of a sentence which is prepared for by a preceding
phrase is preceded by a dash. Example: I am anxious to interview one person — the news editor.

Expressions introduced by such words as 'namely', 'for
instance' and 'for example', if coming in the middle of
sentences, should be preceded and followed by a dash.
Example: They tried many ways — for instance, towing —
before they could get the car to start.

Interrogative expressions coming in the middle of sentences
should be preceded and followed by a dash. Example: We
are — are we not? — all members.

A dash is often used for effect. Example: And after all this
worry we get — what?

TITLES

A London magazine editor said to me once: "Ninety per
cent of the manuscripts that pass through my hands bear titles
that beg for an immediate rejection slip." Another told me: "I
seldom look beyond the title and the first paragraph. If these
fail to interest me, I rarely do more than just scan the rest."

So you see, titles are almost as important as the

45

articles themselves.

It is too much to say that a first-class title will sell a poor article, but it is not too much to say that a fairly good article may sometimes be rejected on account of a clumsy title.

Many papers stand or fall by the titles of their articles. The more these attract, the greater the circulation. Editors know this and pay great attention to titles in consequence.

Film companies assess the value of titles very highly. Some years ago, I knew of an author who sent, to one of the leading American companies, a story bearing the title *The Merry Wives of Reno*. The company found the story unsuitable, but the title was very much to their liking, and for this alone they paid the lucky author over a thousand pounds!

What is a good title? I would define it this way. A good title usually consists of *a few words, put together in an original form, giving a fair indication of the contents* of an article.

Notice particularly the words in italics. They are the important parts of the definition. There should be brevity, originality and aptness.

I have used the words 'usually consists' advisedly, since there are some editors who favour long titles. One of these, for example, was the editor of Competitors Journal. I sold several articles here, and two of the titles I used were: *Cards can lead to riches, poverty or even MURDER* and *£525 Prize that launched an Industry — The Christmas Card Story*. You must get to know the habits of the various editors you are hoping to serve, and study a few copies of their magazines, so that you will have a good idea of the sort of titles which are favoured.

In the light of the definition I have given, consider these examples. They are titles which have appeared above my own articles, at one time or another.

Film Laughs are no Joke

Do you Need a Baby's Love?

Stars Hitched to a Waggon

The first had to do with the cost of film comedies in terms of cash and human suffering; the second with child adoption; and the third with the caravan experiences of well-known stage and screen stars.

If you examine each of these titles carefully, I think you will agree that each is original and that it gives a fair indication of the contents of the article for which it forms the label.

None of these titles was thought out in a couple of minutes. I often spend as much time evolving a title as in writing the article itself. But I am convinced that it pays.

The average beginner would have given these particular articles titles like the following:

What Film Laughs Cost

How to Adopt a Baby

Stars and Their Caravans

Do you not see how commonplace such titles are? There is nothing in them which attracts. They certainly give an indication of contents, but that is as much as you can say. If anything, they give too great an indication. That is not wise. Good titles withhold just sufficient to whet the reader's appetite.

When you find it difficult to evolve a good title, seek the aid of alliteration. Writers of novels frequently resort to this device, and if you think for a moment, you will remember scores of such titles — *Nicholas Nickleby, Rob Roy, Pickwick Papers, Count of Monte Cristo, Pride and Prejudice, Woman in White,* to mention but a few.

I have often thought that the best title I ever evolved myself, based on alliteration, was one which I used quite early in my career. At that time, I was visiting various film studios fairly frequently, and on one such occasion a certain member of a film company gave me some information which I was able to write up into an article which was, I suppose, very daring for those days. Now it would seem quite commonplace. I titled the article *Selling Souls for Screen Success.* It is easy to imagine what the contents were like, and I had the satisfaction of seeing my title placarded all over London.

Whenever possible avoid the use of 'The' at the beginning of a title. Not only is it clumsy; usually it is unnecessary.

Many editors — particularly those of House Journals, for instance — prefer straightforward titles, and you should get to know your market before you work out your title. I have just had an article published in an up-market magazine, for example, which is simply titled *Unusual Golfing Feats.* This title tells the reader exactly what he can expect to find in the article. For a popular periodical I should probably have taken an unusual fact and used that as the title. In this instance, I might have made my title *An Eight-year old boy has holed out in one,* or *Playing golf from Ludgate Circus to Trafalgar Square for a wager.*

COPYRIGHT

I think I should say a few words now about copyright especially since, in recent sections, I have referred to the use of cuttings. You are quite at liberty to use facts contained in different cuttings, but you must never use a whole paragraph — or even a sentence, for that matter — just as it stands. Mix the facts together as much as you can and then present them in language which is entirely your own.

What is copyright? To whom does it belong? When is it

48

infringed? These are but three of the many questions connected with it which are liable to crop up at some time or other in the experience of every writer.

Every piece of original literary work committed to paper is copyright, and the copyright is invested in the person who produces it. Even the letters you write to your friends are copyright and, legally speaking, you alone have the sole right to reproduce them.

In British law, original writing becomes copyright as you commit it to paper, and it is not necessary to register it at any place, or do anything whatever, in order to claim the copyright as your own. You acquire the copyright automatically.

It follows from this that every article you write is immediately protected by the Copyright Acts, and that you, alone, have the power to authorise its use. When you submit an article to an editor, however, you imply that you are willing to grant him a licence to publish your article, and, unless there is any agreement to the contrary, he is at liberty to do this, providing he pays you the rate usually paid by his paper for similar contributions. But he must not go further. He may not, for instance, allow your article to be reproduced in another periodical without your permission.

It sometimes happens that one editor asks another editor for permission to reproduce an article, and when this is done a fee is always offered for the privilege. The editor who first published your article will ask if you are willing to accept this fee, and you will probably wish to do so since it means extra payment for no additional work. But you do not have to agree.

The owner of a copyright may do as he pleases with it. If he wishes he may dispose of it entirely. If he does this he has no further claim in respect of it. It is like having a taxi. All the time the taxi is yours you can keep hiring it out and draw an income for the use of it. Once you sell the taxi to another party, however, you have no further claim in respect of it, however much money it earns in its useful life.

Copyright in all written work lasts for the lifetime of its creator and for fifty years after.

Very often an editor will ask for full rights or all rights. When this is the case, and you accept the fee offered, you must remember that you have parted with all further interest in the work. Is this worth while? Generally speaking, yes. (Here, of course, I am thinking more particularly of short articles). The average short article is seldom saleable in more than one market, and nothing is to be gained, therefore, by refusing a cheque simply because the editor has asked for the copyright. He does not do this because he hopes to make something out of your work, but because he does not want to see articles which have appeared in his paper appearing a little later in some other one. Most editors like their publications to be exclusive.

You will find that some papers print a clause regarding copyright on the backs of their cheques. It is important that you read this before endorsing the cheque. In such cases your signature is more than an endorsement — it serves to sign away your copyright, in as far as the clause specifies.

If an editor publishes your article, and does not ask for full rights (or there is no clause on the back of the cheque to that effect), it is taken for granted that all he has acquired has been first publication rights. This means you are at liberty to offer your manuscript, without alteration, to another editor — providing you mention the fact that it has already been published once. There are some editors who will buy manuscripts which have already been published; but they are few and far between, and when they are found, their rates of payment are usually very low.

If you become a writer under a 'contract of service' — that is, join the staff of a newspaper or periodical — the copyright of your work becomes invested in your employer, unless you have a definite agreement to the contrary.

Ideas and information cannot be made copyright . . . only the manner in which they are expressed. This is a very important point to bear in mind. It means that you are at liberty to take facts from any published article or book and use them in your own articles and books — providing you present them in an entirely different form. You must not lift whole passages, or even paraphrase whole passages. Providing you take the facts only, and clothe them in your own words, you cannot be held guilty of infringing a copyright.

I do not hesitate to state that the majority of the facts given in this section I am now writing have been gleaned from other sources. In no way, however, does this section resemble any of the six sources from which the facts have been derived. The majority of articles which appear in print would not have been possible if the authors had not been at liberty to use facts and ideas already mentioned by other writers.

TRADE PAPERS

"No section of the Press is so badly served as the Trade Press."

"Few aspiring free-lance journalists realise that the easiest market in which to earn frequent modest cheques — which, in the aggregate, can be quite appreciable — is the Trade Press. While trade papers are not actually short of material, they are all crying out for reliable correspondents, and the freelance who is alive can make a fairly steady income from easily picked-up paragraphs, with a good sprinkling of specials and interviews."

These statements are taken from articles which appeared some time ago in *World's Press News,* and my own experience testifies to the truth of them. In fact, I have gone so far as to state, in an article, that "it is my belief that any writer who can work up a connection with a dozen or so papers, published in the interests of various trades, can make a comfortable living. And it is by no means as difficult to work up such a connection as one supposes!"

Any trade of any standing has its own paper or papers. Thus, *Building, Building Design, Building Products Monthly,* and upwards of fifty other publications cater for the construction industry; *Confectionery Production, Baking Industries Journal,* and half a dozen more cover the baking trade, whilst *Computer Management, Data Link, Data Processing* and another ten magazines cater for the computer market; and so on.

There are, literally, hundreds of trade papers. A list of the largest is given in the Second Workshop Manual — *1,333 MARKETS.*

What are the chief requirements of Trade Press editors?

First and foremost, they want news — news of any kind connected with persons engaged in the trade covered, particulars of building schemes, new branches, advertising campaigns, and so on.

News connected with persons covers a wide field and includes deaths, weddings, police court reports, civic activities, staff changes, presentations, changes of proprietorship, and so on.

52

How can news of this kind be obtained?

I will let you into a secret! Until you become known as an accredited correspondent (and are thus able to call regularly on the heads of the various businesses covered, and get your information first hand), you will find that many useful news items can be picked up from your local paper.

You can easily follow up these reports, interview the people mainly connected with them, and write up a new story accordingly.

Two important points to remember about these stories are that they should be crammed with facts and should contain a good sprinkling of names. Trade Press reports are like newspaper reports in this respect. Ordinary everyday police court reports are of little interest to an editor. If, however, someone connected with the case has something interesting to say, or an interesting point arises, then the report becomes valuable to him.

The best way for a beginner to break into the Trade Press is, I think, by first submitting personal items of general interest. When submitting an item, enclose a letter asking if the editor has a representative in your district and, if not, whether you could act as such for him. Few trade papers, if any, are represented in every district, and it will probably not be long before you are able to link up your services with several of them.

Do not make the fatal mistake of thinking that you can act for two papers covering the same trade. If you attempt to do this, it will not be long before you are acting for neither.

As soon as you get authority from an editor to act as local correspondent, have some visiting cards printed with your name on and the name of the paper you represent. These will serve as a useful introduction to persons connected with the trade covered. The next thing to do is to see as many of these persons as possible, tell them you are representing such and such a paper, and ask them to give you any information which might be of interest to an editor. You may not strike much oil at first, but continue to pay occasional visits (at respectable intervals) and as you get known, you will find your lineage increasing.

Some editors allow — and even encourage — their local correspondents to become subscription agents. This means that you leave a voucher copy of the paper with any member of the trade, who is not a subscriber, and if a subscription order follows you receive a percentage of it. An agent usually receives a percentage on all renewals as well. Once you obtain a subscriber to a paper, therefore, you may draw a commission in respect of his subscription over a number of years.

Earlier in this section, I pointed out that what the trade paper editor requires, first and foremost, is news, and I have endeavoured to show how any enterprising freelance can meet this demand.

News, however, is not the only requirement. Every trade paper publishes a number of special features and these are more often than not the work of local correspondents. Ideas for such features usually come when chatting with persons in the trade. For instance, Mr. Blank may tell you he is about to open a new branch. "And that," he adds proudly, "is the third within four years. Ten years ago I had that tiny shop in So-and-so Street. After a couple of years I moved here, and when the new branch is opened I shall have four shops in the County."

"A jolly fine achievement, Mr. Blank," you reply, (that is, if you have your wits about you!). "To what, chiefly, do you think you owe your success?"

If Mr. Blank is the man he usually is he won't be long before he satisfies you on this point, and when you have shaken him warmly by the hand, and got home again, it won't take you long to dash off a thousand or two words telling exactly why he is so successful in business. The result will be a first-class feature which will sell at sight to the editor of the paper covering Mr. Blank's trade.

Sometimes you can pick up an idea in connection with one trade which can be adapted to two or three others. This means that if you are representing more than one paper you may be able to sell an article on the same subject to each of them.

One day when you are calling on Mr. Blank, for instance, he may just be approving a new lighting arrangement. Mr. Blank has pronounced views on lighting and is keen to air his views. You listen carefully to what he has to say and later prepare a special article dealing with the part lighting can play in the trade followed by Mr. Blank. Use of this idea does not end here, however. When you call on persons connected with other trades you can collect their views and thus prepare specials for other papers.

The rate of payment for paragraphs and special articles is not high, but once you get a connection they are easy to write. News is usually paid for at so much a printed line. Special articles command a fee depending upon their length and nature of contents, but it is usually lower than one can expect from the more general magazines.

Most trade paper editors welcome illustrations and if you keep a camera handy, you can add considerably to your income by supplying photographs with your news paragraphs and special articles.

You can often write articles for trade journals even if you do not take an active interest in trade journalism itself. Let me give you a personal experience to show what I mean.

Some time ago I was sitting in the establishment where I always have my hair cut, awaiting my turn to go into the chair, when I began to think: "Why do I come here to get my hair cut? In what way does this particular hairdresser appeal to me? There are three other hairdressers in the town but I always come here. Why?" Thinking along these lines, I built up in my mind a short article under the title *Why I like my Hairdresser.* I thought of all the genuine reasons why I came, and thought of two or three others which might make his service even more appealing to me. When I got home, I typed out my article and sent it to the editor of *Hairdressers' Journal.* The article appealed to him and he published it very quickly.

I thought then, "What is good enough for one trade may be good enough for several others." So I began to map out a series of articles on the same lines, but appealing to different trades. *Why I like my Outfitter* I sold to *Men's Wear; Why I like my Chemist* to *Chemist and Druggist;* and, with the help of my wife, *Why I like my Butcher* to *Meat Trades' Journal.*

On another occasion, I remember, I mugged up an article on the valuable advertising space which was available on the average delivery van, and this subject, again, was exploited in several different markets.

No doubt you, yourself, can think out examples of a similar kind, and they are well worth thinking on if you can.

HOUSE JOURNALS

House Journals are magazines published by business firms either (1) as staff journals giving interesting personal notes about various members of the staff; or (2) as publicity periodicals of a general nature; or (3) as a combination of both.

My experience of these journals is an interesting one. It can be summed up in three short sentences. They are difficult to find. They are usually in need of material. Their rate of pay is high.

One finds House Journals in the normal way only by stumbling across them, but a list of some of the most vigorous in categories (1) and (3) appears in the second book in this series of invaluable Workshop Manuals — *1,333 MARKETS*.

It is impossible to say much, in a general way, about these magazines, since the requirements of one often differ very widely from the requirements of another. The best thing to do is to send for two or three specimen copies and study them carefully. Note particularly whether it is part of the editorial policy to publish only such contributions as have a direct, or indirect, bearing on the firm's goods or services; or whether it is merely to entertain and leave the advertisement pages to 'speak for themselves'. If in doubt, a courteous letter of enquiry to the Editor, asking if he is open to consider outside contributions and for details of the type of thing he favours, will usually bring an interesting reply.

Payment offered by these magazines is usually very good, and sometimes it is exceptionally good. Moreover, "payment on acceptance" rather than "on publication" is very often the rule. Sometimes an editor will ask the writer to name his own fee. When this has been the case in my own experience, I have always replied that I am willing to accept a fee which the editor thinks the particular feature is worth and which his budget allows him to pay. I have always added a few details of payment I have received from other similar journals. In this way I have often been offered a fee higher than one I should have been prepared to ask myself.

Once you get to know a few editors fairly well — and they, in their turn, have a good idea of the kind of material you can produce — you may find that you are frequently being given commissions for special work. When these commissions arrive, like a bolt out of the blue, they are very much appreciated. I have been writing now, at varying intervals, for a quarterly magazine published by a firm specialising in Metals. Whenever the readers of the magazine ask the Editor for an article on a special subject, or whenever the Editor, himself, has what he thinks is a bright idea, he writes to ask if I can prepare an article on the subject. *Making a Will, Calendars, Surnames,* and *Halloween,* are examples of articles I have been able to write and sell in this way.

The Editor of an Engineering quarterly prepares, from time to time, issues slanted to a special subject. When he does this, he writes to ask if I have an idea for a related article. Recently, for example, he produced an issue with an agricultural interest, and wrote to ask if I could do a general article on some aspect of agriculture, or even on the countryside in general. I suggested *Wildfowl Reserves* — of which there are now more than 200 in various parts of Great Britain, taking up several thousands of acres — and the idea immediately appealed to him.

An editor of one House Journal who does not accept outside contributions in the ordinary way, always takes two articles of mine, with a Christmas interest, for publication in his December issue. He has been doing this for some years. I wrote to him once, suggesting an article, and he replied that he had no opening for articles of that nature but that he might be able to use one or two articles of general interest for his

Christmas Issue. I have been supplying him with Christmas features regularly, ever since.

Thinking of House Journals generally of late, has given me an idea which might prove of use to some readers. New industries are springing up these days almost everywhere, and it is not a bad idea to take a look round your own district to try and find a progressive firm which, at present, has no House Magazine, but which could perhaps be persuaded, with your help, to start one. I have looked round my own district and have found one such firm which I think may eventually be persuaded to publish a yearly magazine or perhaps, a quarterly.

The object of House Magazines should be mainly, (1) To help bind the staff closer together by giving interesting news concerning them — such as weddings, outings, and so on — and also by fostering an even better relationship with the management by telling them a little of what is happening, and about the plans for the future; (2) Creating a prestige value between the firm and its customers and potential customers, by giving them some impression of the firm's general activities, and of their relationship with their staff.

Before approaching a management, it is as well to work out a rough estimate of the cost of a magazine you are suggesting. First of all, get a rough idea of the cost of printing a magazine of the type you have in mind. This is best obtained, not from a small local printer, but rather from one specialising in the production of magazines, and whose name can be found in the Printing Trades Directory in your local library. To this estimate you must add the likely cost of the blocks to be used and an editorial fee of, say, something like £100, plus fees for any matter you may have to obtain from outside, other than material collected from the management or its employees.

Nowadays, more and more firms are publishing two

59

separate House Journals — one of interest solely to the staff, and the other in the form of a publicity magazine of wider interest. It will pay you to keep an eye on House Journals. There is no easier way for the average free-lance writer to pick up extra money than by following these markets.

TOPICAL ARTICLES

By 'topical articles' I mean articles which have some bearing on events which are in the news.

It is part of the policy of every editor to keep his paper up to date. Accordingly, many of the articles he prints are directly related to an event which is, or which is expected to be, in the public mind at the time his paper appears. We all know it is impossible to place an article on Easter Customs except for publication at Easter time. And what is true of outstanding topical events is also generally true of events which are only mildly topical.

It is often possible to give a topical twist to an article of a general nature. When this is done the article in question has a much better chance of being accepted. An article on curious wills, for instance, might go to several editors and then not be accepted. If, however, the newspapers publish an account of a well-known person who has died and left a will containing some unusual clauses, the article is easily made saleable by using an opening paragraph centred around this account.

An article is half-way to success if it has a topical opening.

In the days before I was kept as busy with my writing as I am now, I always had by me a number of 'stock articles'. The interesting part about these was that they had no opening paragraphs; they all began on page two.

Every morning I went through my newspaper carefully, and directly I came across a news item which could be used to form a topical opening to one of my stock articles, I lost no time in using it and, within a very short time, my article was in the post.

Speed counts a great deal where topical articles are concerned, and rejection may sometimes be due to no other reason than that an article arrived too late. It pays, therefore, to dispatch by the earliest post possible.

There is no reason why every writer should not follow the method I have just described. It only means rising a few minutes earlier, and if a useful news item is found, you can post the article on your way to business. It is a glorious feeling, trotting off to catch the 8.15 with the knowledge that you have very likely earned a pound or two before breakfast.

You will not, of course, find usable news items every morning, but if your supply of stock articles is a good one, there is no reason why you should not average three or four a month. Anyhow, try it!

PRACTICAL ARTICLES

There is a bigger demand than ever today for practical articles — articles which describe, in a simple way, how to make and do things. "Do it yourself" is now a common phrase, and as man's leisure time increases — as it most certainly will — it will become more and more common. Several men even build their own houses in these days in their spare time and quite a number spend leisure hours making pieces of furniture. As a result of all this interest, more and more publications devote some of their space to printing practical articles; and there are quite a few publications which cater exclusively for the person who wants to know how to do things.

For the purpose of examining the demand for practical articles more fully, let us divide publications into the following four groups — (1) Juvenile, (2) Domestic, (3) Trade, (4) General.

Into the first class fall all those magazines and annuals which are published to interest boys and girls up to the age of 17 or 18, and the children's sections of various newspapers — especially provincial ones — and a few of the weekly and monthly journals.

All young people like to be doing things. Editors know this and they are, therefore, always pleased to consider practical articles. Length may be anything from 200 to 2000 words and sufficient photographs or pen-and-ink drawings, to explain the text, should accompany each article.

To give a list of suitable subjects would need several pages of this book. There are thousands of them. You have only to look around you to find them. There are many everyday things you can write about, providing you treat them in your own way.

Here is an illustration. I was once turning out a cupboard and came across an old box-kite which had brought me hours of pleasure as a boy. I had not made it — it had been bought for me — but when I came to examine it I could see that a box-kite was by no means a difficult thing to make. So I set about making one of my own. It was not an elaborate affair — I did not spend much time over it — but it proved satisfactory, and I knew then that I could write an interesting article about it.

Not worth the trouble, you say? Well, apart from the fact that the kite took me no more than a few minutes to construct, and cost only a few pence, I managed to place four articles dealing with the construction of a box-kite — to an annual, a newspaper, a weekly and a monthly.

Providing you allow a fair time to elapse between submissions, and re-write your article in each instance, there is nothing to prevent you from sending practical articles, on the same subject, to a number of different markets. Do not imagine that because you have written one short article on a certain subject you are not at liberty to write on that subject again. I have met more than one freelance who has been under this impression.

When writing practical articles for juvenile papers be very careful to make your explanations as simple as possible. It is best to assume that the reader knows nothing at all about the subject you are handling. Pay special attention to your diagrams; these should be as near self-explanatory as possible.

If you do not feel competent enough to make good drawings and diagrams yourself, I would suggest you get in touch with Messrs. C. G. Edwards, 26 Fell Mead, East Peckham, Tonbridge, Kent. This Studio produces excellent work of all kinds and its fees are very moderate. Moreover, the directors are very friendly and are always anxious to give all the help they can to the freelance.

Into our second class fall the weekly and monthly magazines which are published for the housewife and the home. There are a lot of these and the editors are always looking out for hints and suggestions which will interest or entertain the housewife or which will make her home more attractive or more convenient.

There are plenty of openings in these domestic magazines

for illustrated articles of the "how-to-do-it" type, but it must be borne in mind that only first-class illustrations are considered. This fact, however, need not keep any writer from trying these markets — no matter if he is a poor photographer, or has never taken a picture in his life. If an idea appeals, an editor will often arrange to have her own pictures taken in the firm's own studio or by a leading photographer.

The number of illustrations and length of manuscript, depend largely upon the market. Generally speaking, it can be assumed that the cheaper magazines favour lengths up to about 750 words, with one, two or three illustrations; whilst the more expensive magazines take lengths up to 1500 words, or even longer, with any number of illustrations up to eight or ten.

Publications which fall into the third class are those published in the interests of various trades.

Editors of trade journals, almost without exception, are glad to consider practical articles, in keeping with the trades covered by their titles. Especially are they pleased to see articles likely to help their readers to produce better goods, make more sales, or become more efficient.

It is not necessary to be directly connected with a trade in order to write articles about it. I have proved this over and over again, and have written numerous articles about trades which do not interest me in the least. The information contained in the articles, however, has been good — otherwise it would not have found its way into print.

How have I obtained this information? Simply by keeping my eyes open and not being afraid to ask questions. I see as much as I can of every shop I go into, and if anything strikes me as being original, I endeavour to get the proprietor to talk to me about it. If it is some sort of gadget he has made himself, or a brilliant advertising idea he has thought out himself, he is usually only too willing to do this. At heart, all men are egoists!

Editors of trade papers like their contributions to be short — available space for matter other than news is usually limited — and generally prefer pen-and-ink illustrations to photographs. If, however, a single photograph almost explains itself, it stands a good chance of acceptance.

Into the fourth class falls a variety of newspapers and magazines, the majority of which publish practical articles only at odd times.

The outstanding exception is the gardening press. I suppose, by rights, this should have been put into a class of its own, for the papers published in the interests of gardeners are largely composed of practical articles — articles which describe how to grow flowers, vegetables and fruit, or how to make useful gadgets for use on the land. If you have anything at all interesting to say you will find that these papers are some of the easiest to break into. Articles should be kept short, and the illustrations should be pen-and-ink drawings, rather than photographs.

Payment made by the gardening press is seldom the highest in journalism but, as pointed out in the previous paragraph, it is by no means a difficult market to enter. Here again, if you are not a gardener, you have only to keep your eyes open in order to come across hundreds of subjects likely to meet with acceptance. For instance, I came across a man once who was using a special home-made dibber. It was different from other dibbers in that it could be used either with a flat bottom or a pointed bottom. I made a pen-and-ink sketch of it, wrote 200 words about the making of it, and sold the contribution to a popular weekly gardening paper immediately.

It is impossible to give a list here of all the publications which fall into this fourth class, partly because there are so many of them and partly because editorial requirements are constantly changing. It can be said with safety, however, that every editor is willing to consider practical articles — providing they are in close keeping with the title of his publication.

Into this class can also be put the wide variety of publications which cater for hobbies, sports, games, and so on — such as, for example, *Yachts and Yachting, Car Mechanics, Canal and Riverboat Monthly, Ski.*

ANNIVERSARY ARTICLES

Anniversary articles are closely akin to topical articles. These are articles which are topical, at some time or other, every year. I refer, of course, to those dealing with events like Christmas, Easter, Boat Race, Budget, and so on. It is a good plan to make a speciality of these, since the same subject can be written up year after year for different markets. Collect as many cuttings as you can, on each event, and prepare your article well in advance.

It is a good plan to make a list of these anniversaries. Here are a few to give you a start.

January — New Year (the Romans commenced the year in March; Mohammedans date their time from the flight of Mohammed, and so on); Twelfth Day (dating back to the time of King Alfred); Plough Monday (the Monday following Twelfth Day); Festival of St. Hilary (13th January); St. Agnes Eve (19th January); Pantomimes.

February — Shrove Tuesday (there are several interesting customs connected with this); Chinese New Year's Day;

St. Valentine's Day; St. Bridget's Day.

March — Boat Race; Grand National; St. David's Day (1st March); St. Willen's Day (3rd March); St. Patrick's Day (17th March). Lady Day. Easter can also be included here although the Festival, of course, occurs more frequently in April.

April — April Fool's Day; Festival of the Passover; St. George's Day (23rd April); Distributing the 'Maundy Money' (given by the sovereign to a number of old men and women); Sinking of the Titanic (15th April).

May — Opening of Cricket Season; Cup Final; May Day; Beating the Bounds; Empire Day: Industrial Sunday (towards the end of the month); St. Dunstan's Day (19th May); Pigeon Racing; Sheep Shearing commences; and Royal Academy Exhibition.

June — The Derby; Irish Derby; Grand Prix de Paris; Ascot Week; May Week (at Cambridge); Longest Day; Festival of St. John the Baptist; St. Barnabas Day (11th June); Battle of Waterloo (18th June).

July — Dominion Day (1st July — a great day in Canada); Independence Day (4th July — a great day in America); St. Swithin's Day (15th July); St. James's Day (25th July); Goodwood Races; Race for the Dogget Coat and Badge (on the Thames); Lord's Week; Festival of Our Lady of Mount Carmel (first Sunday following 16th July).

August — Cowes Week; Harvesting; Festival of St. Bartholemew (24th August); Royal National Eisteddfod.

September — Yom Kippur (a well-known Jewish feast); St. Matthew's Day (21st September); National Brass Band Festival; Highland Games; Hop-picking; Michaelmas Day.

October — Cider Making; Colchester Oyster Feast; Harvesting of Peppermint.

November — Guy Fawkes' Day; 'Shooting Stars' are seen

67

regularly in the middle of the month; Armistice Day; Feast of Martinmas (11th November); Lord Mayor's Show; St. Clement's Day; St. Catherine's Day.

December — Christmas; Festival of St. Nicholas (6th December); St. Kenelm's Day (30th December); Smithfield Cattle Show; Founder's Day at Eton; the 'Halcyon Days' (the days between 14th and 28th December).

I am often asked when is the best time to submit anniversary articles. It is important to know this, since it is very easy to submit them too late. The one fact to bear in mind is that many of the weekly and monthly magazines go to press well in advance of publication date. It is not too early to begin submitting anniversary articles to the monthly magazines four months ahead; and to the weeklies, eight or nine weeks ahead. With newspapers, it is not advisable to work too far ahead, otherwise your manuscript may be forgotten. A week ahead is plenty.

If you intend to make something of a speciality out of writing annniversary articles you will do well to make sure that you obtain *The Writer's and Artist's Yearbook* each September, promptly on publication. This contains an invaluable 'Journalist's Calendar' of Anniversaries and Centenaries for the coming year.

For regular advance news of Events and Festivals in Britain, the forthcoming celebration of Old Customs, and so on, you should obtain *Britain : Events*, a quarterly publication put out by the British Tourist Authority, 4 Bromells Road, Clapham, London SW4 0BJ (Tel. 01-622-3256).

This will supply you with at least thirteen weeks prior notice of scores of newsworthy happenings. Single copies, or annual subscriptions, can be obtained by writing to the British Tourist Authority Sales Office at the address given above.

Christmas articles deserve a section to themselves. There are probably more openings for articles dealing with this world-wide Festival than for any other subject one could name. Many newspapers and magazines publish special Christmas numbers, the majority publish enlarged numbers, and magazines which remain staid and heavy throughout the rest of the year, brighten up their pages and introduce seasonable features at Christmas time.

I know one freelance who concentrates entirely on Christmas stuff and makes a good living from it. He said to me once; "I have come to the conclusion that every newspaper and magazine published, no matter for what class of reader it caters, is worth trying with Christmas features." My own experience endorses this.

It is advisable to submit Christmas articles well in advance. Most of my own articles are always with editors by July — whether the publications are weekly, monthly, quarterly, or yearly. If I am sending anything to Holly Bough, I send as early even as January or February, since this publication usually closes for press early in the spring. It must be remembered that quite a few Christmas Numbers are on sale towards the end of November, and most of them, therefore, close for press well in advance of this date.

In case you are still thinking about my friend who writes nothing else but Christmas features, and are wondering how on earth he finds sufficient subjects to occupy his time, let me suggest a few. Maybe these will set you to work and enable you to sell many articles of your own.

Christmas in Other Lands — A number of articles can be written on this subject, each article confined to one country —

or you can write two or three general articles, containing references to several countries — or the way people in different countries treat one particular part of the festival (the Christmas tree, for example).

Games, Tricks and Puzzles — Articles dealing with these subjects find a place in scores of newspapers and magazines, particularly House Magazines — carefully drawn diagrams must be included when necessary.

Christmas Cards — How they originated — some outstanding designs — romance connected with them — where they are printed.

Presents — Many articles can be written on how to make home-made presents, and offered to the domestic weeklies and juvenile papers — suggestions for presents also make acceptable articles — attractive ways of packing presents is another good angle from which to approach the subject.

Santa Claus — Who was he? — how is he regarded by children in other lands? — think, too, about the men who impersonate him at the big stores — what would you do if you were Santa Claus?

The Christmas Table — There is good scope for practical articles describing how to arrange the Christmas table in an attractive manner — experiment in this direction, using candles, fruit, crackers, flowers, etc., and photograph your experiments.

Carols — How they originated — stories connected with their writers — carol singing in olden times.

Post Office Work —Christmas time is the busiest time of the year in the Post Office, and numerous articles can be written about the way the work is carried through — get some posting tips from your local postmaster — interview a temporary postman.

The Law at Christmas Time — There are all sorts of things we mustn't do at Christmas, that is, if we are to keep strictly within the law. We mustn't watch a football match, for instance, or eat a mince pie!

Parties — These are in full swing round about Christmas time, and hosts and hostesses are often at their wits' end to know how to keep guests entertained all the time. Many editors welcome articles on this subject.

Animals at Christmas Time — It is nice to remember these as well as ourselves — in some foreign countries there are special customs connected with animals.

Turkeys — How they are reared — why they have become so popular — how to carve a turkey (I hope I see this article!)

How Famous People Spend Christmas — Members of the Royal Family — stage, screen, television and radio folk — well-known figures abroad, and so on.

Christmas in History — What notable events have occurred on Christmas Day in the past?

Christmas Trees — How the custom originated — growing the tree — decorating them — points to look for when selecting a tree.

Christmas in Olden Days — This subject should provide material for countless articles — how did people travel at Christmas time? — did they eat bigger meals than we do now? (go back to the Middle Ages and you will be surprised at what they did eat!) — what were their chief pastimes? — what was Christmas like in the days of the Puritans?

Children and Christmas — Do not forget that Christmas is the children's time — articles on how to entertain them are worth considering — also child welfare articles in keeping with the season.

Crackers — How did they originate? — how are they made? —

what outstanding crackers have been known in the past?

Christmas and the Christ — In all our preparations for Christmas, and our enjoyment of it, we are apt to forget the central figure behind it all — there is room for several articles written around this theme.

Christmas in the Services — How is Christmas spent in the Army, Navy, Air Force, and so on?

Christmas in Prose and Poetry — What have our great writers written about the Festival?

Christmas in Nature — The countryside and hedgerows.

Holly and Mistletoe — What do they stand for? — when were they first used? — what superstitions are connected with them? — how, and where, are they grown?

Toys — Articles can be written about the toys of yesterday and today — which, do you consider, are the best toys to give to children? — some toys are dangerous — what effects have different toys on the mind of a child?

Haunted Houses — Christmas is the time of the year when we are expected to hear about spooks and haunted houses.

Christmas Catering — There are endless opportunities for well-written articles dealing with this subject.

Christmas Business — What effect has Christmas on the general business of the country? — roughly, how much money changes hands? — how can small shopkeepers increase their Christmas trade?

Christmas sport — Football, hunting, and so on.

Christmas Stamps — Most countries now issue special stamps for the Christmas festival.

This list does not by any means exhaust the number of possible subjects connected with Christmas. It does show, however, what a wide range exists.

BE A CAMERA-JOURNALIST

When a person coins a new word, it is right and proper that he should give a definition to it. Here then is my definition of 'camera-journalist'.

A camera-journalist is a writer who has sufficient foresight to see that writing and photography have much in common and that, by combining the two, he can add appreciably to his income.

That may be the dictionary compiler's idea of a good definition, but then I am not compiling a dictionary. I am setting out to show you how to make money as a writer, and the above description is intended to awaken your interest to the fact that the question of becoming a camera-journalist is one worthy of careful consideration.

I have mentioned this question to several freelance writers, who make a fair income from their writing, and in every instance I have been met with one or two answers: (1) "I cannot afford the price of a suitable camera;" (2) "I am not really interested in photography and know nothing about it."

Let us look more closely at these answers.

"I cannot afford the price of a suitable camera." When I have asked for a price to be named it has invariably been in the neighbourhood of £50 or over. Listen, I, myself, have sold hundreds of illustrated articles and photographs using a camera costing only a pound or two. Generally speaking, the person who does not know much about photography and is interested only in getting pictures of interesting things he may see, in average conditions, is much better off with a cheap camera — especially the easy-to-use camera of today. He will get far better prints, on average, with a cheap camera than with an expensive one. I have owned cameras myself costing several hundred pounds, but this is only because I have known how to use them properly and have needed them for the taking of special pictures.

I once had a large picture on the backpage of the *Daily Mirror* — it was, in fact, the only picture on it — and that was taken with a camera which cost — in pre-decimalised money — just twelve-and-six!

Perhaps now you are beginning to think differently about the price of a camera. If you are, let me settle the question in your mind for all time. It is not necessary to have an expensive camera. In these days of film perfection, it is possible to get excellent results with the cheapest of cameras.

Of the two answers, however, the second is the more prevalent. Many writers possess the mistaken idea that one must be an expert photographer in order to sell photographs. Do not believe it. Very little technical knowledge is needed to produce finished prints up to publication standard. By far the most important thing is knowing what to take. And if you have a good news sense you should have a good picture sense.

As you go around the country, try to take photographs which will gradually build up into a series, and around which you can then write an article. An example of what I mean is milestones — which are becoming fewer and fewer these days — and signposts. When you come across one which is interesting, stop and take a picture of it. It is surprising how frequently you will find them if you are looking for them. Close to where I live, there is a signpost on a main road, with arms pointing in opposite directions but both bearing the inscription 'To London'. The explanation is that, by turning left you can take the old road to the City, but by turning right, and going a little out of the way, you can join up with a new arterial road, also going to the City. An article along these lines might readily appeal to the editor of one of the motoring papers or of a travel magazine.

Similar sets of pictures could be built up of interesting old cottages, of dovecotes, of windmills, of curious inscriptions on tombstones, of Youth Hostels (I have seen photographs which show that some of these Hostels are particularly attractive). Of ancient village signs, of old inns with fascinating historical connections, and so on.

I have already dealt with trade journalism in an earlier section of this book, but I did not say much about photographs. Most trade paper editors, however, welcome illustrations, and if you are camera-journalist, you can add considerably to your income by supplying pictures with your news paragraph or special article.

Get photographs – preferably head and shoulders – of as many business executives as you can, and file them away so that you can find any particular one at short notice. Once you have got a fair-sized collection, you will find it will provide you with a steady income. Photographs of this kind can be used to illustrate all kinds of paragraphs and will be welcomed by most editors.

Shop windows are always worth careful consideration. If you can secure some good pictures and can write interesting captions for them of between 50 and 80 words, they are almost certain to sell. It is not easy, however, to get good pictures of window displays. Here are one or two tips which may help you.

In the first place it is necessary to bear in mind that it is seldom possible to get good pictures of windows which are crammed full of goods. You must not forget that a camera views the whole window at once. This is altogether different from viewing it bit by bit – as is the case when we go shop gazing. It is a good plan, therefore, to stand well back from a window and examine it critically from that position before exposing your film. You will then realise how desirable it is to select windows which have been dressed boldly and simply.

One of the chief annoyances in window photography is the reflection of outside objects on the surface of the glass. It is seldom possible to eliminate all these, but you will find that most of them are cut out if you can tackle the window when it has a fair coating of dust, or when it is drying after a shower. Sometimes you can cut out reflections by moving your position to right or left. At other times you can effect the same change by moving further back, or by selecting a higher viewpoint. If reflections trouble you, it is a good plan to experiment freely until you have found the best possible position.

You will naturally find there are more reflections when it is sunny than when it is dull. If possible, then, select a dull day for your work. If you still cannot get a picture to your liking, try an exposure by the light of the window illuminations at night.

It is seldom wise to send small contact prints to editors. They always prefer enlargements which have been made to at least half-plate size. You can always get these from the firm which does your developing but, later on, you may choose to do your enlarging yourself. This is quite a simple process, and it is extremely interesting work. A good book on photography will show you how to go about it. Once you have bought your enlarger you will find that you can make suitable prints much cheaper than you can buy them, and you can thereby make your free-lance work more profitable. When submitting photographs, always put your name and address on the back and add what caption is necessary. When the photographs accompany an article, you should also add a line indicating the title of the article.

The copyright of photographs differs from that of articles, in that you hardly ever part with it, and the editor does not expect that he has bought it — unless, of course, there is some definite agreement that he has. Thus, you can go on using the same photograph, again and again, in different features. A good photograph can earn quite a lot of money for you, if properly used, over a number of years.

INTERVIEWING

I secured my first interview — without, let me add, any influence — when I was still in my teens. I wrote it up in 600 words and sold it to a popular magazine for ten guineas — which was a good fee in those days. Since then I have interviewed scores of well-known people, and I cannot remember one interview which has failed to yield good results.

There is plenty of money in interviewing for any freelance who sets about the work in a proper manner. The one thing he must not do, however, is to get over-nervous or easily discouraged. Why be nervous, anyhow? The person being interviewed is not an ogre! He won't eat you. And why be discouraged? Failure is a word which need have no place in the vocabulary of a freelance. No, approach your 'victims' with a feeling that all men are equals, and all your interviews will be successful.

Yet I must admit I felt very nervous when I made my way to the famous London theatre where I was to meet an operatic star who was not only very well-known in this country, but also throughout the United States and much of the Continent. Now, I had heard, he was shortly to tour Germany where — I had discovered — his last appearance had been as a young man of much my own age in the concluding tank battles of the last war.

As I have said, this was my very first interview, and several times during my journey to Sadler's Wells I half kicked myself for being such a fool as to write and ask for it. And when at length I was ushered into the great man's presence my legs were sagging noticeably at the knees.

Nor was my self-confidence reinforced by the way he looked at me as I introduced myself. "Who is this?" he seemed to be asking himself. "What have I let myself in for?"

My obvious youth clearly threw him.

"What papers did you say you are representing?" he asked me.

I hadn't named any papers. But I had done my homework. Before I'd written for that interview I'd worked out where I was going to place it. I'd approached several German papers with a taster of the story, and if I could do it justice it was already sold.

Nevertheless, I was so nervous that, for a moment, I floundered. "I . . . er . . . "

Then, in a split second, it came to me. A cut-and-dried philosophy that has never left me since.

You do your homework. You prepare the ground in advance as much as you can, and I certainly had. I could sell this interview to *Der Stern* if I could land it.

You don't let yourself be intimidated by your own imagination. Everyone gets nervous, but you don't let your natural nervousness take hold and run away with you. The person you are interviewing is nervous, too. Possibly more

78

than you are. So do your best to put everyone at ease by relaxing. In any case, one thing is quite sure.

You have a tremendous edge over the person you are interviewing, provided you do your job properly. You are both going to talk about the one subject they cannot resist: the one they really have to let themselves go on if you give them the smallest kind of encouragement.

How can you fail to get a decent interview when, with *real concern* and *real interest,* you are going to talk about *them?*

So I took a deep breath and I told my opera star about *Der Stern* and its millions of readers all waiting to have news of *him.* And I did it briefly. If I hadn't been brief, he would have started — oh, so very naturally — to interview me. Then, as I slid off the answer to his question, I fed him with ones, prompting ones, about the long dead past, his youth and the war.

Pretty soon, I wasn't having to ask him any questions at all. He was just telling me everything, and it was all coming naturally.

I came away with sufficient material for a really good article which, later, my operatic star approved. After signing his name at the bottom of the copy I sent him, he added: 'Just great!' And, as I said earlier, this interview — my very first — taught me an invaluable lesson.

Do do your homework; know as much as you can about the man, or woman, you are going to meet. Don't allow your own imagination to intimidate you; remember the person you are interviewing will be nervous too. So put them at ease and encourage them, with real concern, and interest, and sympathy, to talk about themselves. Fully.

This is the interviewer's art.

Finally, do not make notes during the course of the

interview if you can possibly avoid it. Many people will close up like oysters if they see that everything they say is being taken down. It's foolish to let anything intrude between your subject and the story you are encouraging him to tell.

This does not mean that you should not have a notebook with you. On the contrary, you should never go without one. But do not use it until after the interview; then use it as quickly as you can. Immediately you get away, write down everything connected with the interview you can possibly remember. Not only the actual words spoken but your impressions of the person himself, details of the surroundings in which you found him and so on.

Never destroy any of these notes. It is surprising how often they come in handy.

When you have finished writing up your notes, examine them from every possible angle. A single interview may easily result in half-a-dozen saleable articles. Let me give you an example.

Years ago I went to Glatton to interview Mr. Beverley Nichols. At that time he was making the village in general and his house and garden in particular, quite famous with his popular books, *Down the Garden Path, A Thatched Roof,* and *Village in a Valley.* My main purpose was to get material for an article suitable for *Home Owner.* I got this material and sold the article; in addition I was able to write an article about Mr. Nichols' dog which sold to a dog magazine (I had a bright idea here; I persuaded Mr. Nichols to smear one of his dog's paws with ink and make an impression on paper. I was then able to use this paw mark as a signature for my article); another about his free-lancing experiences, which sold in the form of an interview to *World's Press News;* another about his books, which sold to *Co-operative Magazine;* a paragraph about the garden, which sold to *Home Gardening;* and three gossip paragraphs which were published in the *Daily Mirror.*

Within the last few years telephone interviews have become common, and this method has much to commend it where people who are normally busy are concerned.

It is necessary, when seeking information on the telephone, to concentrate on the voice. In a practical little book titled *Interviewing,* Mr. W. V. Noble says.

"The voice alone can be used to create an impression. By inflexion and variation of tones, the voice has to create for the person at the other end of the wire, a mental picture of the interviewer, and so much can depend on that picture."

It is also necessary to control the voice. In the same book, the author tells of a reporter who was asked to interview a girl who had been elected Rose Queen. In reply to his question asking what were the qualifications of a Rose Queen, the girl informed him that the Queen was always the girl who was best looking and had the most charming personality, adding she had been found to have these qualifications.

The author goes on: "The reporter replied, 'Yes'. The word itself meant nothing, but there was a wealth of meaning in the way he had said it. The girl had spoken vain-gloriously about herself and in a careless moment the reporter had allowed his 'Yes' to mean 'That's what you think. They all say that. I don't believe you're such a beauty anyway'."

Naturally the girl was offended and she answered remaining questions in snappy monosyllables. The reporter got a very poor story, but a rival paper came out with a really good article, full of additional and interesting facts.

WHAT PAYMENT CAN I EXPECT,
AND WHEN?

This is a very wide question and one which cannot be answered definitely, and certainly not within a short space. There is no recognised procedure which is followed by all editors alike.

One of the pleasures of writing is the uncertainty of its rewards. Seldom does the ordinary freelance know how much an accepted article will bring in — until the welcome cheque arrives.

At the time of writing this book, I suppose the average rate works out at something like ten pounds a thousand words. Some editors pay less than this amount, and some editors pay more. When you are lucky enough to turn in some really exclusive matter, or are well enough known to command a high fee for whatever you write, it can be very much more.

The worst paying markets, in my own experience are the religious papers, gardening papers, and a few trade papers. When I say 'worst paying markets' I mean, of course, in comparison with other markets. Many of the more popular magazines and a number of Home Journals and the leading newspapers, often pay as much as twenty-five pounds per thousand words, and over. Whatever you write, and whichever publication accepts it, you can safely think that you are averaging at least three pounds a thousand words.

The actual writing of a thousand-word article should take little more than an hour. If, therefore, you could write steadily through a forty hour week, and sell everything you write, you would command a good salary. But you will not sell everything — unless you are exceptionally lucky — and you will not be able to write steadily for forty hours a week. Some of your time must be given over to the collecting of ideas, and a searching for new markets.

You will see, however, that if you write only a few hours a week, and can learn to turn out good work, you will be earning a useful second income from your writing.

Reproduction fees for photographs vary from £1.00 to £20.00 or more. Bigger fees, of course, are often paid. Especially is this so with the London newspapers. For an exclusive picture of something with a wide and important interest, as much as £500. Few, however, are able to secure a scoop of this kind, once in a lifetime, and the average freelance can seldom expect payment much in excess of normal rates.

Colour transparencies always command a much higher fee than black and white prints, and many editors pay as much as £25 for these as a normal practice.

Photographs usually earn fees apart from the articles they accompany — when illustrated articles are submitted — and payment is made at so much per thousand words of text, plus so much per picture reproduced. With magazines, the payment for article and photographs comes in one cheque; newspapers sometimes settle the two accounts separately.

The way editors pay varies as much as the rates they pay. You will doubtless hear of editors who 'pay on acceptance'; others who 'pay on publication'; and yet others who 'pay by arrangement'.

Payment on acceptance means that a cheque is sent to the author within a few days of the editor deciding to publish it — irrespective of publication date. There are a few leading papers which follow this plan. Among them, for example, are the magazines published by D. C. Thomson & Co.

Payment on publication means that a cheque does not follow until after a contribution has appeared in print. The

London and Provincial newspapers follow this plan, as do also most of the publishers of ordinary magazines.

Payment on publication does not necessarily mean that a cheque follows immediately on publication, but one usually has to wait until about the middle of the month following publication.

The majority of papers have set date for making payments, and it is not advisable to start sending letters, asking for payments due, until five or six weeks have elapsed after publication. Then, if you like, you can send a courteous letter of enquiry; but never address it to the editor. In the majority of cases, payment is none of his business and he will not thank you if you begin to worry him about it. The person to whom your letter should be addressed is the cashier.

When sending a letter of this kind, be careful to mention all the necessary details. Do not say, merely, "I have not yet received payment for the article of mine you published. Will you please look into this and let me have a cheque immediately." The cashier may not take the trouble to find out what article of yours has been published. No, when you write, mention the title of the article, the issue in which it was published, and the page on which it appeared. You will be more likely to get an answer (and a cheque) if you do this.

Another phrase frequently met with, in connection with payment, is 'payment by arrangement'. Some editors speak of it as 'payment according to merit'. This means that the paper has no set rates, but that the editor varies payment according to the value of the contributions he accepts. Usually he suggests a figure, when writing to say he is willing to use an article, and asks the writer to let him know if this figure is acceptable.

It is unwise to worry too much about payment. The thing

to do is to get plenty of manuscripts accepted. You will find then that editors' cheques come along with pleasing regularity — irrespective of payment arrangements.

REGULAR CONNECTIONS

From the time you first start writing, and right through your years of freelance work until you finally retire (if ever you can!), you should always be striving to work up regular connections. These are the life blood of successful freelance writing, and the more of these you can work up, the greater will be your reward.

If you have followed the earlier sections in this book carefully, and have put what I have tried to teach you into practice, you are now beginning to write articles which you have reason to believe are saleable.

Good. Now let me give you a sound piece of advice. If you want to make your writing pay — and without a doubt you do — you must not be, what I would call, a 'spasmodic contributor'. If you are, you will not get very far.

What you must strive to do is to work up regular connections. I mean by this that you must try to get so well known to a handful of editors, that they will come to look upon you as a regular contributor.

It does not follow from this that you will have, or will be expected to have, an article in every issue of a paper; but that you are represented often enough to keep your name fresh in the mind of the editor. When he sees one of your manuscripts on his desk, he should be able to say to himself, "Oh, yes, this is from so-and-so. I have used several of his articles before. The title of this one is attractive. I expect it will be O.K."

How can you get these regular connections? In the first place, do not bombard as many editors as you can think of, one after another, with ideas and manuscripts. Instead, concentrate on a score or so of markets and keep studying them, and submitting your work to them, until eventually you break into them. And once you have broken in — KEEP IN. As soon as an editor accepts one manuscript — send him another. If possible, make it a little better than the previous one.

If you do this, an editor will soon get to know your work and eventually he will come to depend upon you — and you will have made a regular connection.

Let us sum up this advice in a few words and print those words in capitals so that they will more readily impress themselves on your mind:

CONCENTRATE ON A FEW MARKETS.
STUDY THEM. CONTINUE TO SUBMIT
WORK UNTIL YOU BREAK IN —
THEN KEEP IN.

A few points here may be of help.

1. Make certain the markets you are studying are ones for which you are fitted to write. When you are commencing your career as a writer it is most essential to select your markets with care. If you do this you will be saved a lot of heartbreak. Do not aim too high to begin with. Leave out the national newspapers and the popular magazines with enormous circulations. Concentrate on the lesser fry. Competition will be less keen, but in many cases you will find the payment adequate.

2. Make certain outside contributions are accepted. Not every editor is open to consider outside contributions. Some are kept supplied by a regular staff of writers. If you know your subject really well, you might be able to become one of

these regular writers, but it will be necessary for you first to be able to convince the editor that you really do know the subject which he is anxious to cover.

Make certain that payment is made for accepted work. A few editors invite outside contributions but make no payment for anything accepted and published. The requirements of these are not worth bothering about. It may be good practice to write for magazines which do not pay, but it is a habit which should not be encouraged. It is just as good practice to write for papers that do pay — even if your work is not accepted. You at least have the satisfaction of knowing that it might be accepted, and that if it does, payment will follow.

Writing for papers that do not pay may give you a false impression of your capabilities. The standard demanded by such papers is not usually high. The fact that your work appears in print, however, may lead you to believe that it is up to publication standard, whereas, in reality, it may fall very short of this standard as judged by that set by papers which make a payment.

4. Study carefully subjects, style and length required by the markets you are trying to enter. This is very important. In no other way will you get a clear idea of any particular paper's needs. It pays to see copies of periodicals for which you are aiming to write, fairly frequently. If an editor is beginning to accept your work, try and see every issue of his paper as it is published. In this way you will get to know his requirements more fully and you will not make the bad mistake, as is often made, that you are suggesting an idea, or sending a manuscript, on some subject which has just been used. In any case, if you purchase a few extra magazines in this way, they will undoubtedly provide you with some suitable clippings for your cuttings collection. It is important to study lengths

carefully, since some editors are very particular about the lengths they require.

5. Do not pester an editor with letters asking why he does not accept your work. No, for goodness' sake don't! There is no more certain way of getting into an editor's bad books — a thing you must avoid at all costs. Make it a rule never to send a letter to an editor unless a letter is absolutely necessary.

KEEPING ACCOUNTS

Keeping accurate accounts of the cash you receive and the money you spend on your work, is of great importance. Sooner or later the Inland Revenue will want to know all about it — whether you are doing it full time or only as a spare time hobby — and if you are unable to produce proper accounts, you may be called upon suddenly to pay quite a large amount of tax.

Do not ever think it may be possible to deceive the Inland Revenue by not including all the payments you have received. You can never be sure that you will. Even whilst I have been writing this book, I have received a letter from a publisher, telling me that they have received a visit from a representative of the Inland Revenue and that he has picked out several of the payments made by them during the last financial year. Amongst these payments was quite a substantial one paid to me. Presumably, the tax authorities will trace these payments back to make sure they have been included in the accounts. Fortunately, mine has, and I am therefore not worried. Had it not been included, the tax-man would certainly have started to carry out exhaustive investigations and ask innumerable questions. If such had been the case, it might have been a very worrying experience. As it is, I am in the clear and not a bit worried. This goes to show that it always pays to keep proper accounts.

An elaborate system of book-keeping is not necessary. If you get an ordinary Cash Book, you can enter on the left-hand details of all payments received; and on the right-hand page, all money expended. You should be careful to include on this page details of all money you spend in connection with your work. Postages are important, and I find it best to get a pound's worth of stamps at a time and keep them in a separate envelope. I can then use them whenever I need them for letters and packets connected with my freelancing work. When the supply is exhausted, I can replenish it, and in this way I have a series of £1.00 entered in my accounts for postage.

You must also include all your stationery expenses and you are entitled to claim for all books, magazines, and newspapers purchased in connection with your work. You can also include travelling expenses, and the cost of telephone calls. If you have a telephone in your home and use it for in-coming calls as well as out-going calls, you can also include a part of the rental as well as the cost of the calls.

If you combine photography with your writing, you are entitled to include your expenses for films, enlarging, chemicals, and so on.

You need not concern yourself with accounting for VAT unless your turnover from writing is likely to be more than £5,000 per annum.

If you are a full-time writer, or derive a fairly large income from spare-time work, it will pay you to have your accounts audited by a recognised accountant. This may cost you a few pounds but the advice of an accountant may enable you to effect a considerable saving in tax. A good accountant is usually worth more than you have to pay him.

SO TO THE END

. . . And so to the end of the book, and what, I trust, has been pleasant and instructive reading.

In the various sections, we have considered together, the main questions connected with the business of free-lancing. I have endeavoured to show you how to prepare saleable articles; and where to place them when you have written them. I have given illustrations, from my own experience, to guide you.

The rest is up to YOU.

Set to work with a will, determined never to give up, and never to be upset by rejections or disappointments. Do not curse every editor who returns a manuscript, or yield to the temptation to fling your typewriter out of the window and be done with it! Windows cost money to repair, and it is not the time to waste a good typewriter when there are no editorial cheques coming in to enable you to replace it!

Keep ever in the front of your mind the indisputable fact that what matters most in free-lance work is the IDEA. Play up to this, and you must succeed.

Here's hoping you do!